The Reframing of American Education

The Reframing of American Education

A Framework for Understanding
American Education Post COVID-19

DR. TYRONE D. BURTON

Books may be purchased in quantity and/or special sales by contacting the author.

Published by
Mynd Matters Publishing
715 Peachtree Street NE, Suites 100 & 200
Atlanta, GA 30308
www.myndmatterspublishing.com

978-1-953307-06-4 (Pbk)
978-1-953307-07-1 (hdcv)
978-1-953307-08-8 (eBook)

FIRST EDITION

*This book is dedicated to my mom,
Claudette Calhoun Burton Jones, one of the most
extraordinary women I have ever known.*

*On April 17, 2011, while attending the Induction
Weekend Ceremony at Seton Hall University for
Doctoral Students, my brother called to tell me our
mom had died. Having served as a first-grade teacher
for twenty-nine and a half years, she was not just our
mom, she was our first teacher. She instilled in us the
idea that if our minds could conceive it and in our
hearts, we believed it, we could achieve anything.
Therefore, her legacy of excellence, equity, and equality
lives on in me.*

CONTENTS

Introduction 9

Chapter One
Functional Dysfunctionality 19

Chapter Two
Equal And Equitable Funding For All..................33

Chapter Three
The Case Against Standardization........................57

Chapter Four
Reopening And Resocialization…Really 83

Chapter Five
The Clarion Call To Action 113

Special Acknowledgments 151

In the wake of COVID-19, there will undoubtedly be many books, briefs, and articles written about how to navigate remote learning. However, the system of education has not sufficiently served children who are under-resourced academically and socially. This book provides a framework for the posture American education should take post-COVID-19.

INTRODUCTION

Allow me to suggest that racism and COVID-19 are two sides of the same coin. What has become blatantly clear to most Americans since May 25, 2020, is that there are two viruses plaguing our country: racism and COVID-19. Now, while I don't believe education can solve everything, throughout past national crises, the government has relied on education to be a catalyst for change. For instance, when the Russians launched Sputnik in 1957, on May 25, 1961, President John F. Kennedy made his famous "Moon Shot" speech to Congress. He declared that we were in a space race that could ultimately mean the difference between tyranny and democracy.

Similarly, the Civil Rights Act of 1964 hastened the end of legal Jim Crow. It secured African Americans equal access to restaurants, transportation, and other public facilities. It enabled Blacks, women, and other minorities to break down barriers in the workplace. However, this was primarily done by desegregating the schools. (Please note that for the most part, we are still separate and unequal.) Lastly, in 1983, the United States Department of Education declared that we were a "nation at risk" and suggested all of America's ills could be fixed if we simply fixed education. I further suggest, we are still a nation at risk, as evidenced by the two viruses that are so vehemently afflicting our nation. Racism and COVID-19 are both symptoms of the intentional miseducation of a nation.

I had just finished writing what was to be my first book, *More Than A Notion: A Journey in Educational Leadership in the Age of Accountability.* It was to be released in July, but on March 11, 2020, the coronavirus was declared a pandemic by the World Health Organization. On March 13, 2020, a national emergency was declared in the United States. Schools were closing nationwide and it seemed as if we were in an educational state of chaos. So, I felt compelled to delay the release of *More Than A Notion* and focus instead on writing the book you are now reading, which provides a framework for what American education should look like post-COVID-19.

I began writing this book on April 5, 2020. Since then, however, the entire nation has erupted with protests regarding the murders of Breonna Taylor and George Floyd. On May 25, 2020, Derek Chauvin, a white police officer, kept his knee on the side of Mr. Floyd's neck for eight minutes and forty-six seconds. Mr. Floyd was handcuffed and lying face-down. On that day, George Floyd joined a long line of unarmed Black men and women who have been killed by policemen. He was not the first unarmed Black man to be killed by police, but this incident was the proverbial straw that broke the camel's back. There is no vaccine for racism but there is a cure. It is the unity that Americans—we the people—must forge to form a more perfect union. A union that increases life chances for all children by providing them a free and "appropriate" public education.

Since March, educational magazines and journals have been filled with opinion pieces, articles, analysis reports, and a fair amount of political speculation regarding the changes that must take place once schools open and classes resume. Needless to say, education will never be the same, and that may not be a bad thing. One of the many side effects of this pandemic is that it has brought new light to the inequity and inequality that still exists in the hallowed halls of learning institutions in America. We must take this opportunity to move forward and right the systemic and systematic wrongs that still permeate most schools and school districts.

To provide a framework for simply reopening schools and allow students, teachers, superintendents, principals, parents, business owners, and politicians to engage in the same system of education would be miseducation. To read these pages is to fully understand the plight of our current system of education and have the unction to change it. At the end of each chapter, you should *(learn/know)* something, *feel* something, and commit to *do* something

Know: That education is a civil right, and the current system we are using is fraught with gross inequity and inequality.

Feel: The pain of systemic miseducation that leaves most of our children behind.

Do: Urge policy makers, politicians and educational leaders, boards of education to make expedient changes that will ultimately make FAPE a reality for all students.

The Rehabilitation Act of 1973 requires schools to provide a "free appropriate public education" (FAPE) for students with disabilities. While education may be free and public, whether or not it is equal and equitable remains to be quantified. Throughout these pages, I examine the pandemic and how it exposed the gaps in a system that is already fraught with inequity and inequality. We know that a child who is only educated at school is an undereducated child, which is indicative of the gap between the educational haves and have-nots. I also examine past practices in order to provide a framework for a path forward.

Kamala Harris said, "Our unity is in our strength and diversity is our power." Derek Chauvin had his knee on George Floyd's neck for eight minutes and forty-six seconds. It takes five hundred milliseconds, or half a second, for sensory information from the outside world to be incorporated into a conscious experience. That is literally the time it takes to blink. Our minds really are complex computers; however, I want to appeal to your humanity. At the end of each chapter is a chance to reflect. The objective is for all stakeholders to think and rethink about the way we do the things we do by answering the aforementioned three questions. The time allotted to write your reflection is eight minutes and forty-six seconds, which is the same amount of time it took for a policeman to take the life of George Floyd. Use the time to figure out ways to save a life. More, specifically, the lives of children because they deserve the right to live in a just and equitable America. I believe that what Kamala Harris said still rings true today, "A child going without an education is a crime."

My hope is that this book will start a national discussion between stakeholders who are truly interested in improving the lives of all students. I hope to write in a way that touches the heartstrings of parents, policy makers, teachers, administrators, college professors, educational organizations, businessmen, and laity.

The positions I choose to take regarding the reframing of American education are not new. In fact, some of the arguments will sound very familiar—but in the current context of our nation, I believe it is time for us to progress from protest to policy.

We take a lot of pictures in my family. However, the ones we like the most are put in frames and displayed in prominent places around the house. Isn't it amazing how something as seemingly simple as a frame can turn a picture into art or an indelible memory? Frames have a way of providing focus and clarity to any situation.

Education is no different. According to authors and researchers, Boleman and Deal, there are four frames that govern or encompass education.

They are:

- Symbolic (temple)—meaning, purpose

- Human Resource (family)—people, group dynamics

- Structural (factory)—process, task-based

- Political (jungle)—resources, social influence, control, negotiating, power

Each frame offers multiple perspectives and processes, but each presents its own unique challenges. For instance, the **Structural Frame** deals with how organizations and systems operate. This is done by clearly defining roles, rules, goals, policies, technologies, and environmental expectations. The challenge of implementing this frame is properly aligning people, processes, and technology to enhance the structure, as well as being constantly attuned to its needs.

The **Human Resources Frame** deals primarily with how people in the organization interact. More specifically, it addresses relationships, self-interest, needs, feelings, and skills. The challenge in this frame is being attuned to human needs without sacrificing the goals of the organization.

The **Political Frame** deals with power, politics, self-interest, competition, conflicts, and intrigue. The challenges of this frame are developing an agenda, forming coalitions in order to build a solid power base, acquiring good intelligence, and learning how to dispense information wisely.

The **Symbolic Frame** is probably one of the most powerful frames. When used correctly, it inspires people to have hope. For instance, the United States is a symbol. Each state has a flag as a symbol. Symbols evoke passion and speak volumes even when mouths are closed. The challenge is when symbols are used to invoke hate or negative emotions.

It is in the context of these frames that we will examine just how education should reform or reframe itself. The challenge for the reader is using the knowledge they have gleaned to move from protest to policy.

In Chapter 1, we will discuss the system of education and how it is structured, noting that educators do not control education—government does. We may not be able to effectively change the way the system is structured, but we can elect passion-driven leaders. We need to reframe how and who we choose to lead, which involves the Political, Structural and Human Resources frames.

Chapter 2 highlights the challenges and prevalence of inequity and inequality in education. Related issues are funding, teacher equity, and connections. Inequity and inequality can be fixed if we allocate money to support schools and build alliances with institutions that support this effort. This involves the Political and Structural frames.

Chapter 3 makes the case against standardization. There are two systems in American education: one for the haves and one for the have-nots, which is perpetuated and exacerbated by standardization. If this country is going to live out the creed of its character and provide true liberty and justice for all, we need to reframe how its citizens are educated and assessed. This is the zenith of the Political frame.

In Chapter 4, we focus on reopening schools with an emphasis of resocialization. Many of the schools in our country serve students who are under-resourced academically and socially, which means they need more emotional support. The pandemic has served to more deeply traumatize these students, and I suggest a reframing of school staffing. The Structural and Humanist frames are necessary to make these changes.

Chapter 5 is a clarion call for action. We must reframe our commitment to quality education for all students. All four frames (Political, Structural, Humanistic, and Symbolic) are at play here.

Remember, at the end of each chapter is an opportunity for you to reflect by writing what you have learned (Know), how it made you feel (Feel), and what actions you can take to begin the reframing process (Do).

FUNCTIONAL DYSFUNCTIONALITY (SYSTEM OVERLOAD)

"Every organization is perfectly aligned for the results that it gets."
—Arthur W. Jones

I was on a flight home after a wonderful work week with an elementary school in Pensacola, Florida, when I received word that my company had suspended travel for the remainder of the school year due to the coronavirus. Little did I know that our lives would never be the same, and that what we once considered normal would be no more. Phrases like "remote learning," "distant learning," and "virtual learning" would become a regular and necessary part of our educational vocabulary. This virus that has most of the world in lockdown, or as school folk say,

"In School Suspension (I.S.S.)," or "The Reset Room."

Even now, as schools explore various ways to reopen, the problem is that education is accustomed to one-size-fits-all solutions, i.e., the No Child Left Behind Act of 2001, and most recently, Common Core. It is this one-size-fits-all mindset that has caused a system overload in education, and it is so ingrained in our profession that we have become experts at functioning in perpetual dysfunctionality. Allow me to go a little deeper.

If you commit to a rigorous exercise routine to lose weight, but still eat unhealthy foods, you will probably not lose weight. You can't out-train a bad diet. Activity and progress are two different things. Activity may masquerade as progress, but only progress gets measured results.

> The educational system is full of activity, but has made very little progress.

Systems are living organisms designed to perpetuate themselves. Our system is fractured to a point that it cannot function, and unfortunately, we have adapted to functioning in the dysfunctionality. For instance, education is primarily a state function, and it is governed by the National Governors Association (NGA) and the Council of Chief State School Officers (CCSSO). The Council of Chief State School Officers is a nationwide, nonprofit organization composed of public officials who head the departments of elementary and secondary education, five U.S. extra-state jurisdictions, the District of Columbia, and the Department of Defense Education Activity. The National Governors Association, the bipartisan organization of the nation's governors, promotes visionary state leadership, shares best practices, and speaks with a collective voice on national policy. Founded in 1908, the National Governors Association is the collective voice of the nation's governors and one of Washington, D.C.'s most respected public policy organizations. Its members are the governors of the fifty-five states, territories, and commonwealths. NGA provides governors and their senior staff members with services that range from representing states on Capitol Hill to developing and implementing innovative solutions through the NGA Center for Best Practices.

Education is controlled and run by the NGA and CCSSO—i.e., the governors.

Governors appoint the state superintendent of education. District superintendents are elected or appointed by their local school board. District superintendents appoint school-based and central office staff leaders. Teachers are hired, or in some cases, recommended by principals. The president appoints a secretary of education, but their role is to assist the president in executing education policies and implementing laws enacted by Congress.

One of the problems with the reopening of schools is that the federal government failed to implement a balanced comprehensive plan for reopening. The other problem with reopening is that the government did not take the necessary precautions to control the spread of COVID-19. The NGA and CCSSO gave general guidelines and recommendations to districts, but the plans for each district had to be developed at the district level. This wouldn't be a problem, except the system of education is accustomed to a one-size-fits-all approach for most things, and that size is normally dictated by the NGA and CCSSO.

We practice a one-size-fits-all approach in standardized testing, college placement, college readiness, and funding. The fact that neighboring school districts, less than ten miles apart, may have different reopening plans is disconcerting to most people, but that is our new normal.

WHO IS DRIVING THE BUS?

The most formidable problem, in my opinion, is not that each district has to develop their own reopening plan—it's that the wrong folks are driving the bus. Education is like most businesses—we tend to hire people we know and trust at the expense of hiring someone that actually may be the best person for the job. Our rationale is called the "best fit," which is a legitimate method used in human resources. Let me hasten to say that I have no problem with leaders hiring people they trust. It happens all of the time, but the litmus test for keeping the job is the result (provided they get the necessary help and support to be successful). If that person doesn't get results, they need to be replaced. Hiring is a process that must involve several components aside from the interview. It must take into account the person's ability and capability to effectively do the job based on their work history. Not everyone that has leadership ability necessarily has leadership capability. Likewise, a leader may have the authority or position to get something done but not the power or influence to get it done. Leaders must be hired that possess the authority and power to get the job done.

When George W. Bush enacted the No Child Left Behind Act in 2001, it was based on a business model. This is why we have charter schools—to supposedly promote competitive growth in the market of education. The difference is that in business, individuals who do not reach their goals are repurposed, displaced, or fired. In education, the product is people, which is much more complicated. There are so many variables that are beyond the immediate control of the person in charge, be it the teacher, principal, or director. The amazing thing is that in most cases, even in the toughest schools, we get the job done. The downside—as long as the job gets done, we tend to keep leaders that aren't as productive. I was once at a conference where a principal said there were only two kinds of people at his school: teachers and folks who support teachers. What an amazing mindset to have! Likewise, I believe district leaders should have a similar mantra by stating that in their district, there are only two kinds people: principals and folks who support principals.

PASSION-DRIVEN LEADERS

Allow me to suggest that we hire and elect people who are passion-driven, rather than those who are the best fit. Think of leadership as a continuum going from procedural to conceptual, with these five levels running the gambit of the continuum. "Procedural" means that you have a basic understanding of how things are done. "Conceptual" means you own the process.

Procedural   **Conceptual**

Position•Permission•Production•People Development•Passion-Driven

Position. People respect you because of your position. Your influence will not exceed beyond the lines of your job description. The longer you stay, the more likely you are to burnout and/or leave the profession. Your colleagues begin to limit you and put fences around you. You can't stay in the position more than two years.

Characteristics of a leader at the Position Level:
- Reports to work and other functions inconsistently; they are sometimes late and sometimes early. If burnout sets in, a high rate

of absenteeism will start to occur, as well as addictive behaviors.

- Below average to average job performance, depending on the day of the week.
- Doesn't consistently inspect the performance that they expect from their employees.
- Productivity varies depending on the type of employees who show up to work that day (performance regression can take place at this level).

Permission. People want to respect you and will do so beyond your stated authority. This level allows work to be fun. Staying too long on this level without promotion will cause highly motivated people to become restless.

Characteristics of a leader at the Permission Level:
- Reports to work on time and attends professional development opportunities outside of those offered onsite.
- Sees consistent job performance from those they lead.
- Routinely inspects tasks done by those they lead.

- Has inconsistent growth or organizational achievement.

Production. People respect you because of your reputation in the community and they respect the company for being good. ("Good" meaning your employees enjoy coming to work and have a sense of ownership and pride regarding the organization's performance). This is where most leaders see success. Your colleagues respect you and what you do. Problems are fixed with very little effort because of momentum. Don't let the momentum stop.

Characteristics of a leader at the Production Level:
- Reports to work and other related functions on time (and occasionally shows up early).
- Attends offsite professional development events and leads professional development onsite.
- Sets high expectations for themselves and their leadership teams.
- Is driven by company data most aligned to productivity.
- Gets consistent results year after year (barring systemic or organizational barriers).

People Development. Your colleagues and others respect you because of what you have done for them, and you have an established reputation in the community for consistent success. This is where long-range growth occurs. Your commitment to developing people as leaders will ensure ongoing growth to the organization. This is also where some colleagues will start to resent your good works. Do whatever you can to achieve and stay on this level.

Characteristics of a leader at the People Development Level:

- Consistently reports to work and other school functions early. They stay late and work weekends. Even when they are at home or out shopping, they are thinking about ways to improve their organization and its employees.
- Leads site-based professional development, but are sought after at district, state, and upper management levels to lead professional development. They serve on various committees that affect growth and success.
- Keeps excellent records of assessment data, data walls, employee performances, and conferences. They maintain a wholesome

working environment. Their employees own the process and take responsibility for the success of the organization and their peers.

- Consistently has high growth and success in the context of the company's parameters.

Passion-Driven. People respect you because of who you are and what you represent. This step is reserved for leaders who have spent years growing people and organizations. Few make it and those who do are bigger than life!

Characteristics of a leader at the Passion-Driven Level of Leadership:

- Displays all the characteristics of the previous level consistently.

Passion-driven leaders have the ability to positively transform the people around them, resulting in positive results on a consistent basis.

**Your eight minutes and
forty-six seconds starts now.**

CHAPTER ONE
REFLECTING ON THE REFRAMING PROCESS

*"It can be daunting, exhausting, and intimidating
at times but never stop pushing for change."*
—Elaine Welteroth

Know: After reading this chapter, I learned...

_____

_____

_____

_____

_____

_____

_____

_____

Feel: Reading this chapter made me feel...

_____

_____

_____

_____

_____

_____

_____

_____

Do: After reading this chapter, I am committed to the following...

_____

_____

_____

_____

_____

_____

_____

_____

2

EQUAL AND EQUITABLE FUNDING FOR ALL (THE HAVES AND HAVE NOTS: PROFICIENCIES IN POVERTY)

"The miracle is this, the more we share,
the more we have."
—Leonard Nimoy

U nfortunately, the United States has the highest level of childhood poverty in the industrialized world (other than Romania and Bulgaria). There are multiple methods of calculating poverty, but regardless of the method, the results are similar. According to the National Center for Educational Statistics (NCES), the poverty threshold for a U.S. family of four during the 2011-2012 school year was $22,811. This figure was based on official U.S. Census Bureau calculations. More than 22 percent of

U.S. public school children lived in poverty in 2012, compared to 15.6 percent in 2000.

The problem of childhood poverty is growing. In 2010, almost 48 percent of U.S. public school children qualified for free or reduced price school lunches. No other democratic OECD country boasts such childhood poverty statistics. In 2010, childhood poverty in Finland and Denmark was less than 5 percent; in Norway and Germany, less than 10 percent. Those countries continue to maintain childhood poverty below those rates, while the United States is struggling to keep its childhood poverty below 20-23 percent.

Furthermore, UNICEF found the United States ranked twenty-sixth out of twenty-nine industrialized countries in overall well-being of children—just ahead of Lithuania, Latvia, and Romania, but behind countries like Estonia, Hungary, and Slovakia. The cumulative effects of poverty and associated issues, such as stress and frequent illness, coalesce to depress overall academic achievement.

Regardless of which organization calculates the poverty rate, the United States ranks near the bottom of the industrialized world in terms of children living in poverty.

WHY EQUITY AND EQUALITY MATTERS

Equity is achieved when all students receive the resources they need and are prepared for success after graduating high school. Equality in education is achieved when students are treated the same and have access to similar resources.

In 1896, the U.S. Supreme Court ordained segregation, a separation based on the inferiority of one human being and the superiority of another. Segregation was practiced in the educational domain as well as in other sectors of society. The U.S. Supreme Court upheld a Louisiana ruling that denied a Black man the right to sit in the same train passenger car as whites, and declared that the ruling was not a deprivation of the Black man's rights or a violation of equal protection provided in the Fourteenth Amendment. In 1896, the *Plessy v. Ferguson* decision decreed that it was constitutional for states to establish separate but equal facilities for Blacks and whites, with the inequality of facilities in favor of whites widely noted. This ruling stood until 1954, a time of burgeoning civil unrest that strained the political and economic relations between the U.S. and other countries. In 1954, the U.S. Supreme Court decided in *Brown v. Board of Education of*

Topeka that legal segregation of public accommodations, including de jure segregation of educational institutions, was unconstitutional. As was the case when the U.S. Constitution was amended in the 1800s, numerous efforts (e.g., "white flight" from public schools, laws to limit the U.S. Supreme Court decision) were made to reinstate the status quo that reflected the racial ideology of the 1600s.

Harvard University's Civil Rights Project examined segregation patterns in K-12 public schools from 1991, the year the Supreme Court permitted districts to end desegregation plans, to 2001. The project indicated that in 2001, on average, a white student in the U.S. attended schools in which 80 percent of the student body was also white. A Black student in the U.S. attended schools in which only 31 percent of the student body was white. As declared by the U.S. Supreme Court in 1954, segregated schooling continues to be inherently unequal—a state reminiscent of the pre-Civil War and post Reconstruction eras.

After decades of attempting to achieve racial equality and racial equity in education, these goals remain elusive in the United States. Educational inequality and inequity have emerged and reemerged in various forms throughout U.S. history. There are overt acts of prohibiting education, as well as more subtle manifestations (such as inadequate instructional facilities or scant course offerings, with people of color more likely to be subjected to these conditions). As the populace becomes increasingly diverse, with 2009 U.S. Census data indicating that non-whites will constitute 54 percent of the population in 2050, educational equality and equity for all is more important than ever. For a substantial portion of the population to be inadequately educated in the twenty-first century is not only antithetical to the democratic ideals upon which the U.S. was founded, but is also materially disadvantageous for United States' international competitiveness, global prominence, and quality of life. The demographic shift to greater diversity is already evident.

Let me make it plain. It's been over sixty years since the U.S. Supreme Court declared education "a right which must be made available to all on equal terms." In ruling that separate was not equal, *Brown v. Board of Education* forced federal, state, and local governments to open public schools to all children in the community. The decision marked a huge victory for the civil rights movement. Yet integrating school buildings would prove to be just the first step in an ongoing journey toward educational equity in the nation. There are still structural and social barriers to making a world-class public education "available to all on equal terms." In addition, our ideas about equity have evolved to encompass more than the right to attend school. Advocates are increasingly concerned with allocating resources that will equip all students for success after high school, recognizing that some students require more support than others to get there. This has led many to view equity as adequacy—that is, the principle that all students should receive an adequate education.

For example, consider a district that has a policy of hiring one reading specialist per elementary school. Everyone would agree that this is an equal distribution. However, School A has fifteen students who are reading below grade level, whereas School B has 250 below grade level readers. Equal distribution is therefore not providing adequate services to the children in School B, because the needs in that school are obviously much greater.

The U.S. is a much more diverse nation than it was at the time of the Brown decision. In 1960, 85 percent of the country was white. The largest minority group, African Americans, represented 11 percent of the total population. Asians, Hispanics, and Native Americans represented less than 5 percent combined. Today about 63 percent of the total population is white, and is expected to be less than half by the year 2050. The demographic shift is most evident in our public schools, where children of color are already the majority in the western and southern regions of the U.S.

Childhood poverty has also increased. In 2000, 17 percent of children under eighteen lived in families below the poverty level. Today, that is 22 percent. In addition, the percent of English language learners in our schools has increased over the last decade—from 8 percent in 2001 to 10 percent.

FAIR FUNDING...REALLY

The Education Trust reports that in 2012, the poorest districts in the nation—those in the bottom quartile—received $1,200 less per pupil than the wealthiest, top quartile districts. The national figure conceals large differences by state. The poorest districts in six states received at least 5 percent less than their wealthy counterparts; in Illinois, they received nearly 20 percent less. However, the opposite pattern was seen in seventeen states. The poorest districts actually received at least 5 percent more per pupil compared to those with the lowest poverty rates. Poor districts in Ohio, Minnesota, and South Dakota received about 20 percent more.

Most experts agree that an equitable distribution of education dollars would consider the extra costs involved in districts with high proportions of low-income students or students with special needs. Weighted funding formulas count pupils based on need in order to achieve equity. The federal Title I formula, for example, is based on a calculation that assumes educating low-income students costs 40 percent more than the basic per pupil allocation. The Education Trust repeated its analysis of funding inequity using Title I's formula. When adjusting for the additional needs of low-income students, the analysts found that the gaps were, not surprisingly, wider than when comparing dollar to dollar. In high-poverty districts, per pupil revenues were $2,200 less overall than in low-poverty districts. Moreover, there were twenty-two states in which poor districts received at least 5 percent less than the wealthiest districts, showing that many states still have a long way to go in order to close the funding gap.

Since 1936, Congress has had explicit permission from the Supreme Court to use its spending power to influence state and local action. What federal levers might Congress use to incentivize states and districts to change their disturbing spending patterns? The Elementary and Secondary Education Act has been the primary source of federal education funding and policy intervention since its initial passage in 1965. Congress most recently reauthorized it in 2001 with the passage of the No Child Left Behind Act.

The money that flows through the federal programs authorized by these two laws is only 8.2 percent of all education spending. However, this is not an insignificant amount of money: $47.7 billion in 2007–08. Congress has purchased a vote in how schools are run. Federal lawmakers have not been shy about using their carrot-and-stick power to force dramatic accountability and teacher training requirements on schools directly from across the country. Consider the accountability and teacher-quality provisions added to the Elementary and Secondary Education Act by the No Child Left Behind Act.

So, what can Congress do to change state and local spending practices? Title I of the Elementary and Secondary Education Act—Improving the Academic Achievement of the Disadvantaged—authorizes the largest pot of federal education money, and thus carries the most potential for change. Because the money is directly allocated to school districts, it is easier to change district policies than state policies. Congress has always demanded that districts use federal dollars to enhance educational opportunities for low-income students. The federal funding is supposed to provide additional help for schools serving disadvantaged students, not replace state and local funding. Congress included three specific financial requirements to keep districts from using federal funds improperly:

- Federal funds must be used to supplement nonfederal funded expenditures, not supplant them.
- Districts must spend at least 90 percent of what they spent in the year prior.
- All schools receiving Title I funding must provide services to their students comparable to those in non-Title I schools before federal funds are distributed.

The Department of Education claims these requirements are "critical to the success of Title I, Part A because they ensure that the federal investment has an impact on the at-risk students the program is designed to serve—something that would not occur if federal dollars replaced state and local resources that would otherwise be made available to these at-risk students."

But what if the requirements were changed? To do so, we must understand what the law actually says. In order for a school district to receive its formula-based Title I grant each year, the district must show that "services provided in Title I schools from state-and-local funds be at least comparable to those provided in non-Title I schools." The Department of Education states, "The purpose of this comparability requirement is to ensure that federal assistance is providing additional resources in high-need schools rather than compensating for an inequitable distribution of funds that benefits more affluent schools."

Districts can demonstrate compliance with this comparability requirement in several ways. Approximately 80 percent of districts use a method sanctioned by the Department of Education, ensuring that student-to-teacher ratios in Title I schools are between 90 percent and 110 percent of the average ratio of non-Title I schools. The districts can do this within school-level bands—i.e., by comparing elementary schools to elementary schools—or within the district as a whole. If all schools are served by Title I, then every school must have between 90 percent and 110 percent of the district average student-to-teacher ratio.

Districts can also choose to show comparability using expenditure data instead of student-to-teacher ratios. In this case, they report personnel spending equal to the number of teachers at each school and multiply it by the average district teacher salary. This is an accounting maneuver that effectively wipes out experience-based salary differentials received by individual teachers.

Not many districts have tried to equalize spending based on actual teacher salaries, so we have extremely limited information about political pushback or responses from middle class families. But this potential political concern is one substantive reason we should initiate change as the economy begins to improve. We could avoid taking anything away from schools and instead simply direct new money to the higher-need schools. Leveling up avoids the political and policy problems involved with forcing teacher transfers.

In other words, schools that need more funding must get more funding. School-based leaders should be allowed to allocate those funds. Districts also need to secure money from grants and corporations in order to fund struggling schools.

TEACHER EQUITY

The data indicates the following:

- Black, Latino, American Indian, and Alaskan Native students attend schools with higher concentrations of first-year teachers at a higher rate (3 to 4 percent) than white students (1 percent). English learners also attend these schools at slightly higher rates (3 percent) than non-English learners (2 percent).

- Nearly one in four districts with two or more high schools report a teacher salary gap of more than $5,000 between high schools with the highest and the lowest Black and Latino student enrollments.

- While most teachers are certified, nearly half a million students nationwide attend schools where 60 percent or fewer of teachers meet all state certification and licensure requirements. Racial disparities are particularly acute in schools where uncertified and unlicensed teachers are concentrated. Nearly 7 percent of the nation's Black students—totaling over half a million students—attend schools where 80 percent or fewer of teachers meet certification requirements. Black students are more than four times as likely as white students to attend these schools, and Latino students are twice as likely as white students to attend these schools.

- One in five high schools lack a school counselor.

- 5 percent of three million full-time teachers are in their first year of teaching. However, schools serving the highest percentage (top 20 percent) of Black and Latino students in their school district are more likely to employ new teachers. Six percent of their teachers were in their first year, compared to 4 percent in schools with the lowest percentage (bottom 20 percent) of Black and Latino students in their districts.

- Of the nearly five million English learners nationwide, 3 percent attend schools where more than 20 percent of teachers are in their first year of teaching, compared to 2 percent of non-English learner students. In Alaska, Mississippi, and Montana, the gap between English learners and non-English learners attending these schools is more than five percentage points.

- On average, teachers in high schools with the highest percentage of Black and Latino students are paid $1,913 less per year than their district colleagues in schools with the lowest percentage of Black and Latino students.

ATTRACT, RECRUIT, RETAIN

It is vitally important and critically imperative that principals remember how necessary it is to hire highly motivated teachers and train them to be great teachers. Notice I didn't say to hire the best teachers. New teachers often have very little experience, and they probably aren't used to working with students who are under-resourced academically and socially. That's why "highly motivated" is the listed criteria. Most districts have job fairs to recruit teachers, but if that is the only time you try to attract new teachers, you will always be in an instructional deficit.

Districts must proactively and deliberately go to historically Black colleges and universities (HBCUs) and seek new teachers. In some districts, the recruitment team is not reflective of the majority of the teachers and students in their districts. They usually go to historically white universities (HWIs), seeking teachers to work where the population is mainly children of color or living in poverty. And then you have the audacity to be surprised when they leave the profession within three years.

Now, let me talk to the principals. When your school's culture and climate are such that teachers and students love coming to school, you will not have to recruit new teachers; your staff will do it for you. I'm not telling you what I've heard. I'm telling you what I know.

The first thing to remember is "as is the principal,

so is the school." In other words, you are the brand. This means you must dress like you are the principal, and not the coach or custodian. Those are honorable and necessary positions, but when people come on your campus, they need to know that *you* are the principal. You don't necessarily need to be a model for *Vogue,* but you need to dress to impress. Believe it or not, children learn what they live. You have to be the change that you want to see in your students and teachers. This is called the gradual release model:

I do.

We do.

You do.

The other part of branding is communication. Before school, I would greet every student, teacher, and parent with a smile. A little kindness goes a long way. For some students and staff, that was the only "good morning" they got. It is important to also clearly and frequently communicate your vision to all stakeholders. It may change, but it needs to be communicated so teachers, staff, and students share your vision. Some examples of visions and related messages are:

- Believe, Conceive, and Achieve Your Dream
- Better and Brighter Every Day

- We Are Up For It
- Intentionally Awesome
- Building a Community of Lifelong Learners Through the Development of Human Capital

As educators, sometimes we forget how important it is to be lifelong learners (especially if we are new teachers). I am a proponent of job-embedded professional development. The best way to retain teachers is to help them grow by meeting their professional needs. The days of using a canned approach to professional development are far gone. Professional development must be job-embedded (during the school day), relevant (based on the actual needs of the teachers), and have sufficient follow-up and support. I know the current craze is culturally responsive teaching, and I have no problem with that. But let me suggest another path towards developing quality teachers.

Lowell Milken, the founder of the National Institute for Excellence in Teaching (NIET), is often credited with saying, "The single most important factor regarding increased student achievement is the quality of the teacher in the classroom. Good teaching is not an accident. While some teachers are more naturally gifted than others, all effective teaching is the result of study, reflection, practice, and hard work."

One method that has proven to be effective when improving teacher quality is getting teachers to understand the world in which their students live. It should result in "real-world relevant teaching." To do this, I often use Ruby Payne's *Framework for Understanding Poverty*. Even though most of my teachers were Black, all of my teachers came from middle class backgrounds. I bet yours do, too. The problem was not so much getting them to understand the culture as much as it was getting them to understand that people in poverty have a different set of norms and rules. Ironically, Payne did her research on poor whites in the Appalachian Mountains—but the truth is, poverty knows no color. Poor is poor.

Academic efficacy is another key to improving teacher quality. According to research by Hoy and Hoy from Ohio State, this involves efficacy, trust, academic emphasis, and academic optimism. Efficacy is the belief that faculty can teach students how to believe in themselves. Trust is the belief that students, parents, and teachers can cooperate to improve student achievement. Academic emphasis is the enactment of these beliefs. Academic optimism is the uniting of these three practices into an integrated whole. In other words: when teachers trust principals, and parents trust teachers, and teachers believe that all students can learn, it is a greater indicator of increased student achievement than socioeconomic status.

MAKING CONNECTIONS

The last piece of the equity and equality puzzle is making the necessary connections for systemic success. There needs to be a strong partnership between school districts, colleges, and companies that have a proven track record of increased student achievement. Too often, these three only meet when the need arises. By then, it is usually too late. One of the best ways to ensure schools get help is through this venue.

Some districts have a working relationship with a nearby college or university, but they usually don't have one with a results-oriented company unless schools are in danger of failing. On the other hand, most universities or colleges do not have a working relationship with a results-oriented company unless it is grant funded. Similarly, the alliance between a district, college or university and a results-oriented company are seldom formed unless a school or schools are in danger of failing according to state standards. I am suggesting that such an alliance should exits as a preventive measure instead of an intervention.

What better way to erase and eradicate inequity and inequality than by the unifying efforts of these three institutions? One such company is The Rensselaerville Institute (TRI), located in Delmar, New York. Their mission is to increase life chances for children by helping principals become better leaders. TRI works with school districts around the country, and has worked with Chaminade University in Honolulu, Hawaii. TRI has also been referred to as the "Think Tank with Muddy Boots." I must admit, I am biased towards this company because I work for them—but it is a mighty poor dog that won't wag his own tail!

The beautiful thing about this partnership is that there are always teachers and leaders who need more support. Schools may have professional development departments, but often don't have time to delve into the latest research. Likewise, universities and colleges have professors who are familiar with the latest research, but they are more academicians than practitioners. Companies like TRI are often called in by the district or state when schools begin to "fail," or are consistently not meeting their school performance scores. Doesn't it make more sense for this process to work as a preventive measure?

The question inevitably becomes, where does the money for all of this come from. Well, I told you it is time to change the framework. Doesn't it make more sense to spend money on education than prisons?

What better way to support teachers and principals than having districts work directly with universities?

What better way to support teachers and principals than by having colleges and universities work with companies like TRI?

There is a better way. We just have to commit to believing it, accepting it, and working towards it.

**Your eight minutes and
forty-six seconds starts now.**

CHAPTER TWO
REFLECTING ON THE REFRAMING PROCESS

*"Our future survival is predicated upon our ability
to relate within equality."*
—Audre Lorde

Know: After reading this chapter, I learned...

_____

_____

_____

_____

_____

_____

_____

Feel: Reading this chapter made me feel...

_____

_____

_____

_____

_____

_____

_____

_____

Do: After reading this chapter, I am committed to the following...

_____

_____

_____

_____

_____

_____

_____

_____

THE CASE AGAINST STANDARDIZATION

*"The time is always right to do
the right thing."*
—Martin Luther King, Jr.

B y the end of this chapter, I hope you understand that our system of accountability is wrong. It is wrong for our students, wrong for our teachers, and wrong for a country whose true essence is to allow every citizen to have "the inalienable right to life, liberty, and the pursuit of happiness." Now, let's explore accountability in a broader context that includes standardization, as well as the accountability of parents, school boards, administrators, teachers, and informed citizenry.

As it relates to testing, however, this is truly the tail wagging the dog. Imagine you are a cardiologist and your worth is determined by mortality rates. More specifically, the data used to determine your effectiveness is based on the mortality of your patients. Like other physicians, you have spent eight years in school and have completed your residency. On top of that, you are considered a specialist, not a general practitioner—so, you probably spent even more time and money on school. When patients come to you, they are already knocking on death's door. They are sick and need more intensive care. The general practitioner, however, will see a wide range of patients—some are healthy, and some are at various stages of illness. In fact, they will have some patients come only for a routine checkup. They may not have a patient to die for another twenty years. As a cardiologist, your patients come with a chance of dying within five or ten years.

Imagine at the end of every fiscal year, insurance companies rate a doctor's effectiveness by their patients' mortality rate. All doctors are measured using the same data.

According to the World Health Organization, of the 56.9 million deaths worldwide in 2016, more than half (54 percent) were due to the top ten causes of which I will only name the top three. Number three, lower respiratory infection, causes three million deaths worldwide. Number two is chronic obstructive pulmonary disease which also claims about three million deaths per year. Leading the pack as number one is ischemic heart disease and stroke which accounted for a combined 15.2 million deaths in 2016. The data seems to indicate that cardiologists are not doing a good job, but we know that is not the case

STANDARDIZATION'S PAST AND PRESENT

Our current system of testing, standardization, and accountability paints a similarly distorted picture. Standardization as we know it began in 2000 with No Child Left Behind (NCLB), now known as Common Core (CCSS). It was supposed to solve education's problems by holding schools accountable to a set of unproven standards—but more about that later. However, the 2019 National Assessment for Education Progress (NAEP) data seems to suggest that students were better before standardization.

Mathematics Grade 4 Comparing 2017 to 2019

Student Group	2019 Average Score	2017	2009	2000	1990
White	249	0	0	+	+
Black	224	0	+	+	+
Hispanic	231	+	+	+	+
Asian/Pacific Islander	260	0	+	*	+
American Indian/Alaska Native	227	0	0	+	*
Two or More Races	244	0	0	+	*

Mathematics Grade 8 Comparing 2017 to 2019

Student Group	2019 Average Score	2017	2009	2000	1990
White	292	0	0	+	+
Black	260	0	0	+	+
Hispanic	268	0	0	+	+
Asian/Pacific Islander	310	0	+	+	+
American Indian/Alaska Native	262	—	0	0	*
Two or More Races	286	0	0	+	*

Reading Grade 4 Comparing 2017-2019

Student Group	2019 Average Score	2017	2009	2000	1990
White	230	-	0	+	+
Black	204	-	0	+	+
Hispanic	209	0	+	+	+
Asian/Pacific Islander	237	0	0	+	+
American Indian/Alaska Native	204	0	0	*	*
Two or More Races	226	0	0	*	*

Reading Grade 8 Comparing 2017-2019

Student Group	2019 Average Score	2017	2009	2000	1990
White	272	-	0	0	+
Black	244	-	-	0	+
Hispanic	252	-	+	+	+
Asian/Pacific Islander	281	0	+	0	+
American Indian/Alaska Native	248	-	0	*	*
Two or more races	267	-	0	*	0

(+) Score Increase (−) Score Decrease (0) No Significant Change

* Sample size insufficient to permit a reliable estimate.

It is time to defy standardization. The public education community is at a point in the reform misadventure where it is simply time to step back and become evidence-informed and practical with curriculum design, development, and implementation. Many educators have had enough of the hyper-standardization that is extinguishing their creativity, innovation, and passion from their students. The results are in, and standardization has been demonstrated to be a flawed paradigm for public education. Many educators feel the loss of humanizing and democratizing qualities of public school. Many also believe that civil rights have been violated in the process—especially for high-poverty children and their teachers.

THE JOURNEY

Allow me to share how we arrive at the critical point of standardization. A policy-making body (such as a state education agency) develops, copies, and/or purchases a set of curriculum standards that specify expected outputs. Then, it adopts a one-size-fits-all testing program to determine if standards are met. Finally, the policy-making body mandates that public school personnel teach the specified standards and administer the test to monitor student and teacher effectiveness. This approach is known as performance-guarantee policy making.

Frederick Taylor's scientific management principles propelled standardization into the mainstream of American life. The Sputnik launch created further momentum for standardization, which lasted through most of the 1960s. This was somewhat moderated until the 1983 release of *A Nation at Risk* in which the authors cited international test results to support standardized practices. This included determining the coursework required to earn a high school diploma, competency testing at transition points within the K-12 system, teacher preparation programs, and the amount of time spent in school. In response, the Reagan administration unleashed the rising tide of mediocrity upon the public-school system.

Like Reagan, George H.W. Bush connected performance-guarantee standards to economic and national security. The president went on to describe seven areas that national performance goals should address:

"By performance we mean goals that will, if achieved, guarantee that we are internationally competitive, such as goals related to: the readiness of children to start school; the performance of students on international achievement tests, especially in math and science; the reduction of the dropout rate and the improvement of academic performance, especially among at-risk students; the functional literacy of adult Americans; the level of training necessary to guarantee a competitive workforce; the supply of qualified teachers and up-to-date technology; and the establishment of safe, disciplined, and drug-free schools."

These seven areas identified by Bush at the Education Summit eventually became a centerpiece of the president's State of the Union address on January 31, 1990. By then, these had morphed into six specific goals:

"By the year 2000, every child must start school ready to learn.

The United States must increase the high school graduation rate to no less than 90 percent.

And we are going to make sure our schools' diplomas mean something. In critical subjects—at the fourth, eighth, and twelfth grades—we must assess our students' performance.

By the year 2000, U.S. students must be first in the world in math and science achievement.

Every American adult must be a skilled, literate worker and citizen.

Every school must offer the kind of disciplined environment that makes it possible for our kids to learn. And every school in America must be drug-free."

George H.W. Bush was able to transform the ideas presented in *A Nation at Risk* into specific goals that could eventually be legislated. Almost exactly four years after Bush's 1990 State of the Union Address, President Bill Clinton signed the "Goals 2000 Educate America Act (P.L. 103-227)" into law. Bush's six original goals, along with two additional goals, were included to the bill:

"The nation's teaching force will have access to programs for the continued improvement of their professional skills and the opportunity to acquire the knowledge and skills needed to instruct and prepare all American students for the next century. Every school will promote partnerships that will increase parental involvement and participation in promoting the social, emotional, and academic growth of children."

The bill also expanded upon the original recommendation for testing in fourth, eighth, and twelfth grades by identifying specific subjects in which students should demonstrate competency, partially to ensure productive employment in the future.

The law stated, "By the year 2000, all students will leave grades 4, 8, and 12 having demonstrated competency over challenging subject matter including English, mathematics, science, foreign languages, civics and government, economics, the arts, history, and geography, and every school in America will ensure that all students learn to use their minds well, so they may be prepared for responsible citizenship, further learning, and production employment in our nation's modern economy."

The word "competency" was central to how education policy would be shaped going forward and helped add some bite to the prevailing standardized conception of curriculum. It solidified the focus on outputs and performance that dominates the education policy environment today. Unfortunately, competency replaced equity and equality of inputs, resources, and access to quality. Eventually, the Elementary and Secondary Education Act became a weapon of mass destruction against local control, creative curriculum development, and democratic public-school systems. The weapon became known as "No Child Left Behind."

Enter President George W. Bush and his psychometric vision of education reform. Bush explained his vision at the National Association of the Advancement of Colored People (NAACP) annual conference:

"Under my vision, all students must be measured. We must test to know. And low-performing schools, those schools that won't teach and won't change, will have three years to produce results, three years to meet standards, three years to make sure the very faces of our future are not mired in mediocrity. And if they're able to do so, the resources must go to the parents so that parents can make a different choice. You see, no child—no child should be left behind in America."

George W. Bush's vision became the No Child

Left Behind Act of 2001, signed on January 8, 2002.

The next logical step down the performance-guarantee rabbit hole was the adoption of a common set of curriculum standards. One of the main criticisms against NCLB was that it created fifty different sets of expectations with the development of state standards. The lack of CCSS were a highly touted solution to the perceived standardization of curriculum standards and testing proliferated by the NCLB Act.

According to the National Governors Association and Council of Chief State School Officers (NGA and CCSSO), the vendors of the Common Core Standards Initiative, it would fix the problems associated with the standardization policies of the NCLB era. Fifty different sets of standards ensured that all students would be ready for college, their careers, and be able to compete with their international peers.

Although the CCSS has been marketed as a silver bullet "state-led initiative" that was developed by experts and teachers from around the country, its roots sprout from the corporate world, with one of the main players being standardization advocate Achieve, Inc.

Achieve, Inc. was created by the NGA and various business leaders in 1996 during the National Education Summit held by President Bill Clinton. Clinton viewed the corporate world as an ally that could operationalize the full power of Goals 2000. Clinton opened the doors of the United States Department of Education (USDOE) to the corporate world in hopes of improving education for all children.

So how did NCLB and CCSS morph into President Obama's "Race to the Top?" Before delving into those details, let me give you more background information.

TEACHERS LEFT BEHIND

CCSS was far from being an open and democratic process of creation. Stan Karp explains that "the standards were drafted largely behind closed doors by academics and assessment experts, many with ties to testing companies." Anthony Cody found similar undemocratic links between the development of CCSS and the corporate world, as noted below:

"A confidential process was under way, involving twenty-seven people on two work groups, including a significant number from the testing industry. Here are the affiliations of those 27: ACT (6), the College Board (6), Achieve Inc. (8), Student Achievement Partners (2), America's Choice (2). Only three participants were outside of these five organizations. Only one classroom teacher was involved on the committee to review the math standards."

Karp and Cody noted that none of the participants on the standards development committee represented the K-3 teaching spectrum, and K-12 educators were brought into the process at the end to act as a rubber stamp and endorse the privately developed standards. Those who questioned standardization were not represented on the development committees. The lack of K-12 educator input into the actual development of the standards perhaps pales in comparison to the amount of private money used to market them. For example, as of 2013, the Gates Foundation has reportedly spent over 160 million dollars to promote the Common Core, with other smaller foundations spending funds to do the same.

The NCLB Act was so unpopular by the time President Obama entered office in 2009 that he had to make a change without an act of Congress. Congress was not going to reauthorize the NCLB Act early in the president's first term, which precluded any large-scale education policy initiatives. However, Obama was able to secure funding for an education grant program administered by the USDOE. The grant program became known as "Race to the Top."

President Obama used the standardized assumption to push his administration's education agenda. Obama maintained the tradition of connecting economic security to education reform in his introductory remarks about the Race to the Top program:

> *"In an economy where knowledge is the most valuable commodity a person and a country have to offer, the best jobs will go to the best educated, whether they live in the United States or India or China. In a world where countries that out-educate us today will out-compete us tomorrow, the future belongs to the nation that best educates its people. Period. We know this."*

Period! It's that simple. Obama defined the problem as a lagging of academic performance. He concluded:

> *"And one of the benchmarks we will use is*

whether states are designing and enforcing higher and clearer standards and assessments that prepare a student to graduate from college and succeed in life."

In Obama's vision, benchmarks were the guaranteed outputs in the form of standardized test results. He believed these results predicted college and career readiness.

THE PROBLEM

Standardized curricula beget standardized teaching, leaving little room for diverse instructional methodologies. Over the long term, standardization of curriculum expectations leads to subject-centered instruction. This results in a system that forces children to conform, instead of a system built on the premises of developing creativity and meeting the learning needs of the child.

Standardized curricula stunt creativity, innovation, complex thinking, and other skills necessary for an uncertain future. Standardization also leads to fewer students accessing higher levels of education, and has a dampening effect on cognitive risk-taking. The negative influences of standardized education policies and practices have been known for a long time, yet they persist as if it is the only arrow in the education reform quiver.

THE ANSWER

A static one-size-fits-all set of curricular expectations will not suffice. There is no evidence that one set of curricular expectations produce results that correlate to any meaningful academic, economic, civic, or avocational measures.

Curricula designed, developed, and implemented in the twenty-first century must be diversified, pliable, less standardized, and connected to the unique needs and contexts of the students compelled to experience them. They must attend to the multiple needs of economics, civics, and personal development. What should be the content of such curricula? What are the purposes of public school? John Goodlad borrows from Dewey and others when he efficiently describes the underpinnings of curriculum making.

He says, "Rational process of curricular decision making should be guided by a conception of why we have schools [and] what schools are for. Schools should do what the rest of society does not do well and what individuals and society very much need."

Public school has historically had specific purposes centered around the fulfillment of three complementary functions: economic—students experience a general set of knowledge and skills they can use as a platform to progress to specialized education for a vocation and economic development; socio-civic—knowledge and skills that help students gain experience in being responsible and participating citizens in a democracy and the global community; and avocational—knowledge, skills, and experiences that help students develop their personal interest, passions, and hobbies.

The authors of *Adventures in American Education Volume II*, combined the three complementary functions of public school into two categories, and described the purpose of public education to address the needs of the individual and society.

Before I quote the Eight-Year Study, let me hasten to say that I am aware 1942 was not a good year for African American education. We were still separate and unequal. Isn't it sad that we are still separate and unequal some over seventy years later? As we move forward, we must recognize society as a blended community. We must accept the unique needs of various cultures, and not constantly thrive in chaos. We must strive to be the positive change that we want to see in the world.

Now, in this definition of purpose, two broad guiding principles are evident: the educational program should aid the learner in making effective adaptations to their environment in all its major aspects—physical, economic, and social; and the educational program should develop in each individual's personal characteristics that will enable them to participate effectively in the preservation and extension of the culture.

Economic viability and standardization do not have to go hand in hand. One does not beget or need the other. Curricula should be informed by evidence, based on needs of students and the larger society, unstandardized, and multifaceted to achieve the various functions of a public-school system in a democracy.

ACCOUNTABILITY

Now that we have explored accountability and standardization, it is time to look in the mirror. The famous writer Maya Angelou once said, "Do the best you can until you know better. Then when you know better, do better." It is time for us to do better.

Specifically, this means that policy makers (NGA, CCSSO, USDOE, and the president) should make evidence-informed decisions and stop allowing politics to stifle America's most precious resource—our children. These policies always disproportionately affect children in poverty. It didn't matter whether the president was a Democrat or Republican, the policy of standardization never wavered. This speaks more deeply to the fact that the true gap is not an achievement gap, but a wealth gap that keeps the diaspora between the "haves and have nots." Education does not make one poor. It's not about increasing standardization to increase achievement. It's about decreasing poverty so children can take advantage of the education resources they have. Presidents from Reagan to Obama believed standardization would improve America's poor economic standing and performance as a global competitor. Some policy makers seem to think we have been a nation at risk since 1983. They would have us believe the gap-trap theory which refers to all of the smoke and mirrors policy makers use to convince us that we are in educational dire straits. They also use phrases like "wealth gap," "poverty gap," "opportunity gap," and "hope gap." Stop following the trend and follow the evidence.

The evidence suggests something, though. The Martin Institute of Prosperity has published the Global Creativity Index since 2004. A recent index (2015) provided rankings for 139 of the world's countries, including the industrialized countries that make up the Organization for Economic Co-Operation and Development (OECD) members and partner countries. The index includes the nineteen members of the G20 group of nations. All the countries considered to be the United States' competitors are ranked by the index.

Researchers from the Institute compiled data from 2010 to 2014 relative to each country, covering creativity, economics, social progress, and culture. The Institute's researchers used three categories to describe creativity: technology, talent, and tolerance.

The United States ranked second in overall global creativity, behind Australia. Other prominent members of the G20 lagged far behind. Italy was twenty-first. Japan was twenty-eighth. South Korea was thirty-first. Russia was thirty-eighth. China was sixty-second. India was ninety-ninth. The United States ranked third in creative talent, behind Australia and Iceland. Somewhat surprisingly, given the cascade of negative comments regarding U.S. public school achievement, the United States ranked second in educational attainment. These results suggest that whatever gaps exist when students take their standardized tests disappear later.

Now, imagine how well the United States would rank if there were true equality and equity in our education system!

Likewise, administrators at every level should challenge policy and practices that we know are detrimental to our schools and school districts. Politics is a part of education, so embrace it. Use it to increase life chances for children. Stop accepting unfunded mandates just because they are pushed down the system and passed as educational law. Need I remind us that Jim Crow was law, but it was not in the best interest of all Americans and was later abolished.

School boards have a responsibility to their constituents to ensure all students are afforded a right to a free and appropriate public education. That means school board members that represent most affluent communities should be just as concerned with how students are doing in a poor community.

That concern needs to reflect how they vote, as well as the policies they adopt. Schools systems reflect their communities. Wouldn't it be wonderful if schools on the less affluent side of town were funded and supported as equally as schools in affluent communities? It may mean adopting performance-based budgeting, which simply means schools that need the most support get the most support. Support also means equitable staffing and enrichment programs. Enrichment programs like foreign language, music, art, physical education, and gifted classes should be staples in schools where students are disenfranchised socially.

Lastly, parents have a moral responsibility to make sure their children get the best education possible. This means becoming active members of the PTA and attending school functions. It means supporting teachers as they teach your children. Even if there is a disagreement, you should both look at the evidence and agree to do what is in the best interest of your child. It means holding board members accountable for ensuring that students in your district are getting the necessary resources to be successful. It means attending school board meetings. It means talking to your child about the importance of education and leading by example, because children learn what they live. It doesn't matter if you didn't do well in school; make it your mission to say the buck stops with your children.

**Your eight minutes and
forty-six seconds starts now.**

CHAPTER THREE
REFLECTING ON THE REFRAMING PROCESS

"We need to raise the bar, elevate our standards for racial literacy. Because without investing in an education that values both the stories and statistics, the people and the numbers, the interpersonal and the systemic, there will always be a piece missing."
—Winona Guo & Priya Vulchi

Know: After reading this chapter, I learned...

_____

_____

_____

_____

_____

_____

_____

_____

Feel: Reading this chapter made me feel...

_____

_____

_____

_____

_____

_____

_____

_____

Do: After reading this chapter, I am committed to the following...

_____

_____

_____

_____

_____

_____

_____

_____

REOPENING AND RESOCIALIZATION...REALLY

Our deepest fear is not that we are inadequate.
Our deepest fear is that we are powerful beyond
measure. It is our light, not our darkness, that
most frightens us. We ask ourselves, who am I to
be brilliant, gorgeous, talented and fabulous?
Actually, who are you not to be?
—Marianne Williamson

The pandemic forced more than 132,000 K-12 public schools to close their doors, disrupting the lives of more than fifty million students and their families. Reopening schools is the foremost topic of discussion among all school leaders and governors. But for us to reopen and return to the same misaligned system would be miseducation. Nevertheless, this is a situation that we must deal with in real time. Dr. Fauci has said time and time again that there is no one-size-fits-all plan for reopening schools.

The problem is that education has become a business with a one-size-fits-all attitude. It's like one big line dance with everyone dancing to the music of non-educators, who often don't know how the music should actually sound. A truer analogy would be akin to going to a nice club, with a dance floor on the bottom and a balcony up top. The non-dancers can drink, socialize, and view those dancing. The people on the dance floor can only see things from their perspective as they focus on the line leader. Let's call this group the "have nots." On the other hand, we have the people on the balcony who can see the entire dance floor—probably even the entire club, from their privileged perspective. Let's call them the "haves." I am not casting dispersion on the "haves" any more than I am suggesting social shame on the "have nots." I am simply trying to help you understand that one-size-fits-all is one size for a certain segment of our population—which happens to people in poverty, or the "have nots."

When COVID-19 hit and the nation's schools went to remote learning, children in affluent schools never missed an instructional beat. Their music never changed. For the most part, children in this category already had sufficient technology at home and at school. No problems with hot spots there! Class sizes were already small, allowing for almost one-on-one learning to take place. I'm sure really wealthy families had private teachers. On the other hand, children who are under-resourced socially and economically had little to no technology at home. Some, if not most, needed hot spots. Principals and teachers had to learn how to teach virtually overnight, as well as still provide packages for students who did not have access to technology. The same pandemic—two different side effects.

However, there were some districts that serve large populations of under-resourced students and did masterful jobs by making sure the needs of their students were sufficiently met. Kudos and congratulations to the superintendents who were told what to do, but not how to do it and still made great things happen for children. Many also provided feeding sites for students, because they knew the only meal some of their students got was at school. Kudos to the principals who took those plans and made them actionable. Kudos to the teachers who virtually invited students into their homes and still delivered quality instruction. Kudos to the parents who now realize that teachers have an amazingly tough job, and they weren't lying when they said your child was having problems in reading and math. I bet Teacher Appreciation Week will look different next year! You all made an impossible task look easy, but that's what great teachers, principals, and superintendents do.

Now, let's dive into the belly of the beast. As mentioned earlier, Dr. Fauci often states that there is no one-size-fits-all plan for reopening schools, and that we should work in tandem with the public health officials.

THE DILEMMA

Education is a state function, and as such is controlled and regulated by governors. What made education's reaction to the pandemic so seemingly dysfunctional was that the government's priority when COVID-19 really hit was the general public. They had to deal with contact tracing, testing, and the lack of supplies. Most of us didn't know what personal protective equipment (PPE) was until corona came to visit. Governments also had to work with a president who was in denial during the critical months of preparation. It was also made into a political issue, which is why there was a stark difference between how Democrats and Republicans handled the pandemic. I agree with reopening the economy, but instead of focusing on reopening bars, governments should have been trying to figure out how to reopen schools.

In terms of reopening, the Centers for Disease Control and Prevention has given guidelines to states. Governors have created their own guidelines based on the aforementioned recommendations. In some cases, state superintendents have created guidelines for school districts. In turn, local superintendents must create a plan for reopening. It may look different in each district, depending on how the virus has infected each community. However, most district superintendents have a plan that contains one of three versions:

1. Open with students and teachers at school.

2. Open with students and teachers at school, and have an option for virtual school.

3. Open with students and teachers at school on a dual or split schedule.

In some cases, they may do all three. District superintendents will also have to plan for the following in the context of social distancing, contact tracing, disease spread and all of the other challenges that come with COVID-19:

- Transportation
- Sanitation that meets CDC requirements before, during, and after school
- Where to eat breakfast and lunches
- Temperature checks upon entering school
- Extra-curricular activities
- Policy for sick employees
- Policy for sick students
- Technology
- Class size

Notice I haven't even mentioned anything regarding instruction, because there are so many factors school leaders will have to consider. As an example, we can examine the second phase of the Council of Chief State School Officers' (CCSSO) plan, Restart and Recovery.

CCSSO's mission is to ensure that all students participating in our public education system—

regardless of background—have access to the resources and rigor they need. Within days, the CCSSO began working with state leaders to assess needs and provide credible guidance on everything from school closures and remote learning policies to the safe distribution of school meals. They facilitated information sharing and best practices between states and assembled a resources library. Based on what they learned from the leaders on the front lines, CCSSO quickly developed a comprehensive framework to address and respond to COVID-19's impact on the K-12 education system. The Restart and Recovery plan provides guidance and support to states as they plan to restart schools and recover student learning loss.

They provide guidance in four areas: Continuity of Learning, Conditions of Learning, Leadership and Planning, and Policy and Funding.

Their Continuity of Learning framework includes:

- Providing a planning template on the restart of schools, including options for new configurations, blended learning, or staged reopening.

- Providing guidance to measure learning loss, including the use of diagnostic assessments.

- Assisting states on strategies to mitigate and recover learning loss, including through summer programming.

- Ensuring learning supports for vulnerable populations, including students living in poverty, students of color, students with disabilities, homeless youth, and ELs.

- Sharing strategies to provide high-quality instructional materials for all students.

- Strengthening professional development for educators on distance learning.

- Comprehensively and sustainably solving the digital learning gap.

Their Conditions of Learning framework includes:
- Ensuring continuation of wraparound supports, such as school meals and access to counseling.

- Providing guidance on quality childcare for essential personnel.

- Sharing guidance on trauma-informed SEL, including a focus on school culture and climate and deployment of multi-tiered systems of support.

- Sharing healthy and safety protocols for reopening schools, including cleaning, screening, monitoring, deploying school nurses, and more.

- Providing guidance on parent and family engagement and supports, particularly around distance learning and re-opening protocols.

Their Leadership and Planning framework includes:
- Creating comprehensive Restart and Recovery planning templates, including self-assessment tools and opportunities for expert input.

- Providing guidance on contingency planning in the event of virus reemergence.

- Supporting robust communications and stakeholder engagement on COVID-19 response and use of funds.
- Building coherence in response across SEAs through CCSSO's 17 collaboratives and other support networks.

- Providing leadership support for chiefs and senior leaders through one-to-one and small group consultancies.

Their Policy and Funding framework includes:
- Providing guidance and support to states on the most effective and impactful use of federal funding and flexibility.

- Continued advocacy at the federal level, particularly around additional federal resources to address the social and economic impacts of COVID-19.

- Sharing of strategies to mitigate the impact of projected budget shortfalls in states.

- Creating guidance on assessment and

accountability measures, and federal spending under ESSA for the next school year.

- Determining the best strategies to close the digital divide and provide equitable access to devices and internet.

In *Five Things State Leaders Should Do to Ensure Students Have Equitable Access to Learning Opportunities During COVID-19 School Closures*, published by The School Superintendent's Association (AASA), the authors state:

"The Education Trust has monitored states' tireless efforts to support districts, schools, educators, and families to ensure the well-being and safety of all students as the COVID-19 pandemic spreads. While that remains our highest priority, we know that states are beginning to identify the actions to take, in partnership with other stakeholders, to ensure that their most vulnerable students, including students from low-income backgrounds, students of color, English learners, students with disabilities, and students experiencing homelessness, foster care, or engaged in the juvenile justice system, have equitable access to the resources they need to thrive while schools are closed and to ensure action will be taken to address lost instructional time.

In order to best support school districts in allocating local, state, and federal resources to ensure all students have access to high quality learning, we believe states should take the following actions...

Create and maintain centralized, clear, and regular communication to community stakeholders.

- Create a user-friendly, multilingual online hub for families and students to receive up-to-date information and educational resources. The platform should allow families to access links to guidance and materials in multiple languages, as well as to submit questions to state education agencies (SEA) that are responded to in a timely fashion. Beyond online resources, states should consider setting up and advertising telephone hotlines in multiple languages to field questions and concerns or using text message/push notifications to share critical updates.

- Engage directly with community leaders and

organizations to get input and ensure that community needs are met.

Maintain and strengthen critical supports for students and families in need.

- Opt-in to Pandemic EBT to provide access to food for both families who have been participating in the school meal program and those who have not but have a high level of need. States should implement Pandemic EBT so all eligible families seamlessly receive financial support to purchase food without additional application or verification requirements.

- Work with districts to ensure that students who rely on school meals continue to receive them. Districts should make meals easily accessible for students, especially those from low-income backgrounds, including by coordinating multiple meal pick-up points as well as, if possible, meal drop-offs via school bus routes or other transportation partnerships. The state should also collect and make public data on meal distribution by district.

- Work with districts to coordinate supports for students with disabilities, via (where possible and supported by the student's IEP and/or 504 plan) telephone or internet lessons and at-home study and activity packets tailored to student needs and to prepare for a return to school that allows for (a) quickly resuming the provision of special education services and (b) providing additional services to address any learning loss due to inaccessibility of distance learning opportunities.

- Work with districts to coordinate mental health supports for students via multilingual hotlines staffed by counselors, school psychologists, and other relevant staff, and provide lists of resources and supports available to meet students' mental health needs.

Provide guidance and resources to districts on educational services for vulnerable populations.
- Leverage their bulk purchasing power and/or partner with businesses and internet providers to offer laptops/tablets and expanded internet

service in high-poverty communities to enable all students access to distance learning opportunities. See, for example, California's partnership with Google to provide mobile hotspots and Chromebooks to students in rural areas.

- Create and provide resources to support English learners and students with disabilities, including a centralized site that houses high-quality instructional materials and language supports. See, for example, the Louisiana Department of Education's Family Toolbox for Supporting Students with Disabilities.

- Provide professional development for educators to effectively facilitate distance learning. The state can lean on expertise of schools and institutions that already engage in this practice, such as universities or online K-12 providers with track records of success. See New Hampshire Department of Education's database of resources on distance learning for educators, including webinars and self-guided learning series.

- Reallocate and repurpose any unspent state McKinney-Vento and Title I funds to help districts meet the urgent needs of students currently identified as homeless, and families and youth who become newly homeless as a result of the economic crisis.

Support districts to develop plans with short- and long-term solutions to address COVID-19 challenges.

Schools and districts are under enormous pressure to ensure that students' needs are met during the emergency school closures. Some districts have far greater capacity to meet these needs than others, and states should be strategically supporting those with the greatest unmet needs.

In order to ensure all students are meaningfully served, states should require district leaders to make publicly available how they and the schools within their boundaries will address the challenges of extended school closures, especially the following equity concerns:

- How districts will communicate regularly

with all students and families in multiple languages and formats.

- How districts will ensure that students from low-income backgrounds will receive meals, including those who may lack transportation to meal sites, who move frequently, and/or who may be staying outside of the district's boundaries due to homeless or foster care status.

- How districts will support continuity of learning for all students, and specifically, how they will target supports for those who are most vulnerable (students from low-income backgrounds, students with disabilities, English learners, and students experiencing homelessness, foster care, or engaged in the juvenile justice system), including by: a) Addressing inequitable access to learning opportunities during and after school closures, including access to technology and high-quality instructional materials, b) Providing postsecondary transition planning for high school seniors if closures extend through the end of the school year, including providing determinations of independent status for the FAFSA for unaccompanied homeless youth, c) Sharing data about student learning at the end of the 2019-20 school year with parents and families *(without the benefit of having annual assessment data).*

- How districts will address the socioemotional and mental health needs of students both during and after school closures.

- How districts will support and engage educators throughout this period of disruption, including: a. Childcare, sick leave, and telework policies b. Clear guidance on expectations for student instruction and other forms of student support, and a process for obtaining support for students experiencing crisis or in need c. Professional development, especially related to the use of distance learning.

- How districts will explicitly use McKinney-Vento homeless liaisons to be essential personnel and ensure that homeless liaisons have access to the resources needed to continue to identify and serve homeless students, including through new stimulus funds.

- How districts will utilize federal funding through the new stimulus package to meet the needs outlined above.

- How districts will partner with local entities, including both local government agencies and community-based organizations, to meet these needs. States should ensure that district plans are immediately made available to the public and target additional support to those districts with the weakest plans that also have substantial student need. This support could take the form of dedicated SEA staff time to "virtually embed" into the local education agency (LEA) for a short time period, an SEA offer of emergency funding to support a particular need, or an offer for the SEA to create and support implementation of a draft plan on behalf of the LEA if the LEA would welcome such assistance.

Ensure federal stimulus funds are distributed and used equitably.

On March 27, 2020, the president signed the CARES Act, providing additional resources to states and school districts to address challenges posed by the coronavirus pandemic. $13.5 billion has been distributed to states and school districts based on Title I formulas. These funds can be used for a variety of purposes based on the state's unique needs. To ensure these funds are used to support the state's most impacted students and families, SEAs should ensure funds are targeted to schools with the greatest needs. They should also ensure stakeholder input on use of funds and publicly report on, and require districts to report on, how funds are used. We also urge states to use the 10% of funds allowed for state activities on:

1. Creating or expanding mental health/crisis hotlines and other virtual supports that will be critical for students, educators, and school system employees (or laid off employees) and their families around the state.

2. Ensuring that districts that serve large numbers of students from low-income backgrounds have the additional supports and resources they need to meet the needs of their students

3. Direct support for McKinney-Vento liaisons in districts with large concentrations of students experiencing homelessness.

4. Direct support for coordinators of programs for special education and English learners in districts with large concentrations of students with disabilities or English learners.

In addition, $3 billion will be distributed to governors to use on either K-12 or higher education. The CARES Act does not specify how governors must distribute this money but the SEA should ensure funding is targeted toward schools, institutions of higher education, and districts with the greatest needs. SEAs should now begin to think about how to strategically use their state funding streams in coming years to close learning gaps resulting from school closures and ensure all students ultimately meet grade-level standards by supporting students from low-income backgrounds, students of color, English learners, and students with disabilities who had less access to high-quality educational experiences before this pandemic and whose need for support and services is even more urgent now. We sincerely appreciate the continuous efforts across the country to support families through this crisis. We know these are extraordinary times and no single agency or organization has all of the answers. The Education Trust remains ready to support states in any way we can, and commits to being a thought-partner and resource to agencies and organizations throughout the country.

Reopening will be fraught with many challenges, but superintendents, principals and teachers will get it done—and make it look easy.

RESOCIALIZATION

The academic and social regression that some students experience during the summer months is commonly called *Summer Slide* among educators. However, due to the pandemic, when students do return to school, instead of the *Summer Slide* they will have what I affectionately call, "the COVID-19

Avalanche." All students regress in the summer, even with summer school. Great teachers compensate by providing quality instruction at the beginning of the year in order to help students regain lost knowledge and build bridges to new learning. As students return to school, the challenge is going to be how to effectively deal with their emotional trauma.

I could have easily entitled this section "Post Traumatic Stress Syndrome for Children," or "Trauma-Sensitive Schools." Children in poverty often experience all sorts of trauma, most of which is seen as defiance. While the word *trauma* has become something of a colloquial term, the chronic stress associated with severe and ongoing health and education problems is not related to low-level stressors (such as watching a scary movie or getting into a fight with your best friend). As school districts explore trauma-informed practices or work to develop trauma-sensitive schools, a new understanding of trauma is emerging.

The National Institute of Mental Health defines two basic kinds of trauma.

The first comes from a single incident, such as a hurricane or a school shooting. These affect many students or a whole community, and often involve broad community responses.

The second type—a common but often much harder for school staff to spot—is complex trauma, such as chronic neglect, housing or food instability, or physical or sexual abuse.

Complex trauma can lead to so-called "toxic stress," defined as a response to "severe, prolonged, or repetitive adversity with a lack of the necessary nurturance or support of a caregiver to prevent an abnormal stress response." Not all students who experience a traumatic event develop a toxic response. Studies have found those with a strong support structure tend to be resilient.

All of this coupled with what our nation is experiencing is adding to the trauma that our students face, which I believe is causing an Adverse Childhood Experience (ACE). ACE is one of the most popular concepts for understanding and gauging trauma. It uses a set of common examples, such as abuse, neglect, and family problems, that are associated with long-term problems in health, education, and social relationships.

In the long run, those who experienced four or more symptoms of ACE were four to twelve times more likely to abuse drugs or alcohol, engage in risky sexual behavior, or commit suicide, compared with those who did not have traumatic experiences. Additional research suggests that each ACE increased a student's risk of absenteeism, behavior problems, and performing below-grade level in reading, writing, and mathematics.

Here are actions that districts should take as students return to school. The federal Every Student Succeeds Act encourages states and districts to incorporate trauma-informed practices that are evidence-based. Districts can use Title II money to train teachers in the techniques and support needed to help educators understand when and how to refer students affected by trauma, and children with, or at risk of, mental illness as well as training for all school personnel on how to prevent and recognize child sexual abuse.

I once attended a conference where the presenter, an amazingly outstanding principal named Artesza Portee said, "There are two kinds of people at my school: teachers, and those who support teachers." What a profound statement to make. What a profound attitude to have. With all the challenges that teachers will face this coming year, they will need a lot of help and support.

Schools, especially elementary schools, should be staffed accordingly, with the personnel listed below on-site daily:

- Principal
- Assistant principal of administration
- Assistant principal of instruction
- Master teacher K-2
- Master teacher 3-5
- Instructional content coach for ELA social students
- Instructional content coach for math and science
- Counselor
- Response to intervention specialist
- Nurse
- Social worker
- Exceptional learners instructional specialist
- School psychologist
- Behavioral intervention specialist for exceptional students
- Behavioral intervention specialist for regular students
- Parental involvement specialist
- Support staff for small group instruction

- Director who has previously served at a school with a similar student population

Administrative Flow Chart

Principal	Assistant Principal Administration	Assistant Principal of Instruction	Counselor
Assistant Principal of Administration	Social Worker	Master Teacher K-2	Nurse
Assistant Principal of Instruction	Parental Involvement Specialist	Master Teacher 3-5	School Psychologist
Counselor	Behavioral Intervention Specialist Exceptional Students	Instructional Content Coach Social Studies and ELA	Response to Intervention Specialist
	Behavioral Intervention Specialist Regular Students	Instructional Content Coach for Math and Science	
		Exceptional Learner Instructional Specialist	

Lastly, the goal is to have a seamless School-Wide Positive Behavioral Intervention System (PBIS). The process needs to be clearly defined for what works at each school. Schools should also consider adding a layer by using a "RESET" Room. RESET is an acronym for Restoring Emotions Safely, Emphasizing

Trust. Students could be sent there in lieu of in-school suspension as a way to deescalate behaviors.

**Your eight minutes and
forty-six seconds starts now.**

CHAPTER FOUR
REFLECTING ON THE REFRAMING PROCESS

*"Treating different things the same can generate as much
inequality as treating the same things differently."*
—Kimberlé Crenshaw

Know: After reading this chapter, I learned...

_____

_____

_____

_____

_____

_____

_____

_____

Feel: Reading this chapter made me feel...

_____

_____

_____

_____

_____

_____

_____

_____

Do: After reading this chapter, I am committed to the following...

_____

_____

_____

_____

_____

_____

_____

_____

CHAPTER

THE CLARION CALL TO ACTION
(Eight Minutes and Forty-Six Seconds)

*"The essence of America lies not in the headlined
heroes but in the everyday folks who live and die
unknown, yet leave their dreams as legacies."*
—Alan Lomax

T his final chapter is a clarion call to everyday folk,
because at the end of the day, it will be the
everyday folk that will make the lasting change
in our country. That means the doctor and the nurse.
The principal and the custodian. The preacher and laity.
The school boards and the community stakeholders.
The teachers and parents. The CEO, stockholders,
and the secretary. University professors and university
students. The barber, beautician, and the bus driver.
The bottom line: everyday folk includes everybody.

THE VILLAGE AFFECT

As we have seen on the news, protesters are from various backgrounds, cultures, classes, and ethnicities. However, as we seek solutions that right some systemic and systematic wrongs, I want to challenge my village folk. The famous proverb, *It takes a village to raise a child*, originates from Nigerian Igbo culture but it defines what Kamala Harris meant when she said, "Our unity is in our strength and diversity is our power."

In *The Mis-education of the Negro*, Carter G. Woodson writes:

> "One of the most striking evidence of the failure of higher education among Negroes is their estrangement from the masses, the very people upon whom they must eventually count for carrying out a program of progress.
>
> With respect to developing the masses, then, the Negro race has lost ground in recent years. In 1880, when the Negroes had begun to make themselves felt in teaching, the attitude of the leader was different from what it is today. At that time, men went off to school to prepare themselves for the uplift of a downtrodden

people. In our time, too many Negroes go to school to memorize certain facts to pass examinations for jobs. After they obtain these positions, they pay little attention to humanity.

This attitude of the 'educated Negro' toward the masses results partly from the general trend of all persons toward selfishness, but it works more disastrously among the Negroes than among the whites…Such conditions show that the undeveloped Negro has been abandoned by those who should help him. The educated white man, said an observer recently, differs from the 'educated Negro' who so readily forsakes the belated element of his race.

When a white man sees persons of his own race trending downward to a level of disgrace, he does not rest until he works out some plan to lift such unfortunates to higher ground; but the Negro forgets the delinquents of his race and goes his way to feather his own nest, as he has done in leaving the masses…With the exception of the feeble efforts of a few all but starved-out institutions…Negroes have not influenced the system at all in America."

EVIDENCED BASED RESULTS

If historically Black colleges and universities (HBCUs) were on trial today, would there be enough evidence to convict them of helping "the masses?" Let us examine evidence from the February 1997 issue of *The Scientist*.

In the United States, there are more than one hundred HBCUs. In the late 1860s, these institutions were designated by the federal government to educate African Americans as a result of a segregated educational system in the South. Administrators at the majority of these schools view their mission differently from their counterparts at majority U.S. institutions. Rather than focus their efforts and resources on cutting-edge research, they concentrate on undergraduate education. These administrators, along with many observers, contend that this is an appropriate allocation of their resources, particularly in these days of scarce federal research funding.

TEACHING-ORIENTED: The National Science Foundation's (NSF) Luther Williams notes that HBCUs have a strong tradition of stressing undergraduate education.

"HBCUs traditionally have been built around a

mission of undergraduate education," explains Williams, assistant director of the directorate for education and human resources at NSF. "But this does not mean that good, solid research cannot be conducted at these schools. Teaching and research should not be seen as conflicting entities."

INVALUABLE: Former Morehouse College provost, John H. Hopps, points out the educational utility of undergraduate research. Students at Morehouse, for example, participate in several innovative programs designed to involve undergraduates in scientific research. Yet research output is less important than is research for its educational value. He notes that it is considered "a critical teaching tool for undergraduates." He observes that students who engage in scientific investigation side-by-side with faculty gain valuable experience.

An important goal of science programs at historically Black institutions is to provide African American undergraduates opportunities to do quality research that will enable them to continue their education at major research institutions and become part of the next generation of scientists.

Cell biologist J.K. Haynes, chairman and

professor of biology at Morehouse, explains that his college is "oriented to preparing students to go on to graduate school."

"It's not that administrators don't recognize the importance of scholarly research," he adds. "But it's just not as important to the college's mission as is teaching."

DUAL DEMANDS: Many point to the difficulty of wearing several academic hats and also conducting research.

With their primary mission centered on teaching, historically Black institutions often find themselves struggling to obtain federal research funding dollars. The emphasis on teaching puts additional pressure on faculty who are scraping for research grants, acknowledges Shirley Russell, Professor and Chairwoman of Microbiology at Meharry Medical College, an HBCU in Nashville, Tennessee, and Assistant Dean for Research in Meharry's School of Dentistry. The teaching load at an HBCU frequently makes it difficult to be a researcher, she maintains, adding, "If I'm not productive enough, the grants don't get renewed."

Haynes contends that the situation can be a

catch-22. Without sufficient time to do research to obtain preliminary data, scientists cannot hope to compete for highly sought-after R01 investigator-initiated awards from the National Institutes of Health. The situation is even worse for young researchers.

George Hill, a professor of biomedical sciences at Meharry, notes that some researchers at mainstream institutions and members of Congress question the usefulness of spending federal research money on HBCUs as opposed to better-equipped, research-intensive universities.

He maintains that there are three reasons why research at these schools shouldn't be overlooked. First, much of the research focuses on diseases (such as hypertension, stroke, diabetes, and prostate cancer) that disproportionately affect African Americans and other minorities. Second, he argues that many African American undergraduate and graduate students still want to get their degrees in an "environment in which they can relate to a professor or scientist on the faculty. Often students feel they have a better chance of getting a good education and training at such institutions." The third reason for supporting HBCUs, Hill says, is the need to fill the pipeline. By providing opportunities for research and training, "you create a situation for students and young faculty to be mentored. This increases the number of minority scientists for the future."

EARLY START: Florida A&M University's Vice President for Research, Dr. Franklin Hamilton, feels that science students should get involved in research early in their sophomore year.

Many HBCUs are bullish on their future in research. "We encourage students to go into internship programs, to get involved in research in their sophomore year," says Dr. Hamilton.

"We're establishing a greater number of graduate programs, enrollment has increased, and the research base has increased threefold in the last seven years," Hamilton adds.

Today, Howard University is the only HBCU that can be classified as a comprehensive research institution, based on the numbers of doctoral programs it offers. However, several of these schools, such as Meharry, have developed institution-wide research programs in science and medicine. Others, such as Tuskegee University and Alabama A&M, are known for agricultural research. Federal aid and various federal grants and training programs are helping historically Black institutions train future scientists. The NSF-sponsored Centers of Research Excellence in Science and Technology (CREST) provides up to $1 million a year for up to five years— with the possibility to renew for another five—to institutions to support research and help establish a research infrastructure. The program, which awards approximately $8 million annually, aims to increase the number of master's and doctoral degrees awarded to minority scientists and engineers. CREST supports Clark Atlanta University's Center for Theoretical Studies of Physical Systems, for example, and has aided Howard University in establishing a Materials Science Research Center.

Research conducted by Marybeth Gasman and Felecia Commodore from Penn State University on Historically Black Colleges and Universities suggests that while the research on HBCUs has grown substantially over the past thirty years, the body of research still has substantial gaps and holes. If filled, many of these gaps and holes would lead to stronger institutions, greater knowledge on the impact of HBCUs and enhanced learning experiences for HBCU students. Many young scholars are interested in studying HBCUs but are often discouraged: when they approach their advisor with the topic, they are told it is not important and that their career will be limited by the topical choice. There is a lack of support within sections of the HBCU community for research that might uncover weaknesses or not treat HBCUs in an entirely favorable light. We encourage those interested in pursuing research related to HBCUs to find mentors who will support them in their pursuits.

Her research also led her to suggests that it is important for individuals affiliated with and who care about HBCUs to conduct this research before uninformed outsiders do it. There needs to be a concerted effort from HBCUs, HBCU faculty, HBCU scholar-practitioners and HBCU allies—the "insiders" and the "outsiders"—to ensure those closest to HBCUs have the opportunity to share their own voice, rather than simply have others speak for them. HBCU leaders and organizations that ignore negative data and institutional challenges do so at their own peril.

Unfortunately, I did not attend an HBCU but I was raised by a mother that did and as such, I have a heart and passion for the work that HBCU's do. My mother attended what is now Grambling State University and because she was a teacher, most, if not all, of her friends attended either Grambling or Southern University. So even though I didn't attend an HBCU, I was raised in a world of pride and respect for HBCUs. While serving as a principal, I can say without hesitation and reservation that some of my best teachers were graduates of HBCUs.

I attended Northeast Louisiana State University (NLU) for my bachelor's degree, Louisiana State University in Shreveport (LSUS) for my master's degree and Seton Hall University where I obtained a Doctorate in Educational Leadership and Management Policy, all of which I am proud of and fortunate to have, each with its own unique challenges and life lessons. However, I must admit that I am biased because I believe that HBCUs should be the ones leading the research regarding which work strategies and interventions work and don't work with students that are under-resourced academically and socially. They should be the catalyst for instructional change regarding how to turn around "failing schools." I am appreciative, thankful and grateful that Historically White Institutions (HWIs) conduct research on what works in schools but it is time for HBCUs to take the instructional bull by its academic horns.

There was a time, when one of the only things that African Americans could be were teachers and HBCUs cranked out the best. Somehow along the way in our "overcoming" we left teachers behind, thereby leaving the schools and communities they serve behind as well. The truth is, No Child Left Behind didn't start with President George W. Bush, it started with us. If you can't say amen, say ouch! Let me strongly advise again that HBCUs make strong connections with results-driven companies like TRI and transform the laboratory schools on their campuses to be the model for strategies that are effective with students who are under-resourced academically and socially as well as seeking funding sources to do the research and the necessary work and provide some solutions as preventive measures not counter measures.

WHERE DO WE GO FROM HERE?

How far have we really come as it relates to the village helping the village? How far do we want to go? Are we really our brother's keeper? Do we actually hold these truths to be self-evident that all men are created equal? I pose these questions not just to a village, but to all who would see America truly be one nation under God, indivisible, with liberty and justice for all.

As I mentioned in the introduction, my goal was for you to know something, feel something, and then do something.

We who live in the melting pot and social experiment of America need to find a way to embrace the ideals that this country was built on while shunning the blight and sin of racism. If "sin" is too strong of a word, allow me define racism as "a monstrously infectious mindset that causes men to hate people unlike themselves and develop a poisonous passion to kill."

I mean killing in every sense of the word: physically, mentally, psychologically, and emotionally. Carter G. Woodson stated, "If you can control a man's thinking, you do not have to worry about his action. When you determine what a man shall think, you do not have to concern yourself about what he will do. If you make a man feel that he is inferior, you do not have to compel him to accept an inferior status, for he will seek it himself. If you make a man think that he is justly an outcast, you do not have to order him to the back door. He will go without being told; and if there is no back door, his very nature will demand one."

One of the ways to heal is to first accept the fact that there is a problem. As we protest, we need to go through the five stages of grief: denial, anger, bargaining, depression, and acceptance. It is encouraging to see protests now being led by white people (as well as large, diverse multi-racial groups), because it suggests that we are moving past the denial phase into anger. Hopefully, this will quickly lead to bargaining (policy). As much as I hate to say it, white and Black Americans were in denial. Our white brethren didn't want to talk about it. Even though we talked about it, not enough of us were *being* about it.

How else do we explain having in excess of two million African Americans with college degrees, earning almost $600 billion annually, and the African American community is in shambles? How can foreigners make more money in the Black community that African Americans? Why do we only spend three percent of our money with African American businesses? What explains less than thirty percent of American families with internet connection? How can African American families own big screen televisions, but no computers? Which is worse: a

Black illiterate high school graduate, or a Black college graduate who benefitted from affirmative action campaigning for its demise? Again, if you can't say amen, say ouch.

How far have we really come since 1933, when Carter G. Woodson wrote *The Mis-Education of The Negro*? We need to accept that the school-to-prison pipeline is real. According to the U.S. Bureau of Justice Statistics (BJS), in 2018, Black males accounted for 34 percent of the total male prison population, white males, 29 percent and Hispanic males comprised 24 percent.

Race, Ethnicity	% of U.S. Population	% of U.S. incarcerated population.	National Incarceration rate (per 100,00 of all ages)
White (Non-Hispanic)	64	39	450 per 100,00
Hispanic	16	19	831 per 100,000
Black	13	40	2,306 per 100,000

It's a fact that schools are as segregated now as they were in the 1960s. In "Still Separate, Still Unequal: Teaching about School Segregation and

Educational Inequality," Keith Meatto states, "Racial segregation in public education has been illegal for sixty-five years in the United States. Yet American public schools remain largely separate and unequal— with profound consequences for students, especially students of color. Today's teachers and students should know that the Supreme Court declared racial segregation in schools to be unconstitutional in the landmark 1954 ruling *Brown v. Board of Education*. Perhaps less well-known is the extent to which American schools are still segregated. According to a recent *Times* article, 'More than half of the nation's schoolchildren are in racially concentrated districts, where over 75 percent of students are either white or nonwhite.' In addition, school districts are often segregated by income. The nexus of racial and economic segregation has intensified educational gaps between rich and poor students, and between white students and students of color."

In a related article, "How Much Wealthier Are White School Districts Than Nonwhite Ones? $23 Billion, Report Says," Sarah Mervosh states: "School districts that predominantly serve students of color received $23 billion less in funding than mostly white school districts in the United States in 2016, despite serving the same number of students, a new report found."

The report took aim at school district borders, which it said can chop up communities and wall off wealthier districts to fund their schools with local property tax revenue, while poorer districts are unable to generate the same revenue. "Because schools rely heavily on local taxes, drawing borders around small, wealthy communities benefits the few at the detriment of the many," the report said.

The report, which looked at state and local funding for school districts in the 2015-16 school year, found that more than half of the nation's schoolchildren are in racially concentrated districts, where over 75 percent of students are either white or nonwhite. On average, nonwhite districts received about $2,200 less per student than districts that were predominantly white.

School districts are generally funded locally, but states are supposed to fill in the gaps so communities are evenly funded despite wealth disparities. The report showed that in many states, "they are not keeping up with their own obligation," stated EdBuild CEO, Rebecca Sibilia.

Differences in funding translate to the classroom,

where underfunded communities often use older, worn textbooks and have less access to computers, said Francesca López, associate dean of the College of Education at the University of Arizona.

Funding schools equally will not get the job done. Schools must be funded equitably which means schools that need the most help and support, get it. Because education is a civil right, states and local districts must adopt an ideology that all students must have the opportunity for a free and appropriate education. This means that businesses and board members alike must have some financial and political skin in the game. The board member in the wealthy part of town must be as concerned about his fellow board members' constituents on the poor side of town.

I concur with the statement made by Ms. Sibilia who said, "When it comes to education, it is a public good and people need to share their wealth with their neighbors."

Again, where do we go from here?

Now is the time to move from protest to policy. We need to elect people to office whose platform is built on justice, equality, and equity—not just in vain rhetoric, but people who have the track record to prove that they are walking the walk and not just talking the talk. Talk is cheap, and actions have already spoken louder than words. Now, let's go a little deeper and clarify which people we need to elect. I mean everyone who holds an elected local, state and national position. A partial list would be:

- President
- Governor
- Mayor
- Senators
- Representatives
- City councilman
- Alderman
- Parish commissioners
- School boards (local and state)
- District attorneys
- Pastors

As one of the elders in our church often says, now is the time to put some "do-lalujah with your hallelujah." Examine everyone's track record, and if they are not voting to support the rights of all people, vote them out of office.

Educators don't control education; politicians do. As stated in previous chapters, the president sets that national narrative. The laws regarding education are controlled by the NGA and CCSSO. Politicians are often moved to act by either big money (i.e., corporate interest) or a strong grassroots movement.

Now is the time for educational organizations and state and local subsidiaries to have one voice. We could literally change the direction of education in America. Why reopen just to go back to the same system of dysfunctionality that existed? Are we our own worst enemy?

Now is the time for all parents to be active participants in their child's education. In some schools, there are too many parents who only come to school to present a problem. For instance:

- If the only time you come to your child's school is to complain about the teacher, that's a problem.

- If you never attend PTA meetings, that's a problem.

- If you never attend Family Math Night or Reading Night, that's a problem.

- If you never attend Muffins for Moms or Donuts for Dads, that's a problem.

- If you only attend parent-teacher conferences because you were ordered by the court, that's a problem.

- If you never attend school board meetings, that's a problem.

- If your child has been in school for nine weeks and you still don't know the name of your child's teacher, that's a problem.

- If your child has a medical diagnosis of ADHD and you refuse to give them medication but still send them to school, that's a problem.

- If you tell your children you love them but never spend any time with them, that's a problem.

A child that is only educated at school is an undereducated child. True education begins at home. Principals whose population mostly comes from middleclass and upper-class homes will generally have students who fit traditional parameters of a fundamental knowledge base, which is more akin to a general practitioner. For instance, these students will normally enter school knowing their names, their parents' names, and their address (or at least the name of their street). Most have seen and held a book, or have been read to. They might also know basic or primary colors and shapes. If they come from a home where the average income is $150,000, they may have a robust functional and academic vocabulary. If they come from a home where the average income is $50,000, they may have a moderate to average functional and academic vocabulary. Usually, they come from two-parent homes, and have been taught basic social skills (such as the difference between an inside and outside voice, or how to follow basic directions). Their parents also tend to be supportive of the school, and their parents and grandparents may have completed high school or college.

On the other hand, a principal who serves under-resourced (academically and/or socially) students is more akin to a specialist. The traditional term for students in this category is "at risk," but I prefer to use the aforementioned term. Regardless of a child's socio-economic status, when they attended my school, it was a safe zone, meaning they were no longer at risk. When I use the term "under-resourced academically and/or socially," I mean that they may come from homes that fit the definition for generational or situational poverty as characterized by Ruby Payne in her book *Framework for Understanding Poverty*. Generational poverty is defined as being in poverty for two or more generations. Situational poverty is a shorter period of time and is caused by circumstances such as death, divorce, etc. These students often come from households where the average income is less than $24,230, which is below the poverty line. Unlike students with upper class or middle-class backgrounds, they may have a below average functional vocabulary and very little academic vocabulary. They are often very disorganized; for instance, they may lose papers or only complete part of an assignment. Students may also be physically aggressive, or like to entertain.

THE POVERTY GAP

According to the National Center for Children in Poverty, there are more than 72 million children under the age of eighteen in the United States. 32.4 million of these children live-in low-income families, and 16.1 million children live in poor families. These numbers have steadily increased. In 1989, 32 percent of all public-school children were from low-income families. In 2000, it was 38 percent; in 2006, 42 percent; in 2011, 48 percent; and by 2013, the rate crossed the threshold of one half so that low-income students became a new majority in the nation's public schools.

Flores defined the poverty achievement gap as "a problem of unequal opportunities to learn experience by many low-income students and many Latino and African American students." Flores found that poor students from these minority population centers are less likely to have access to experienced and qualified teachers, more likely to face low expectations, and less likely to receive equitable per student funding. In virtually every place where these gaps have been studied, there is a strong correlation between students' literacy and the social elements of poverty.

While poverty is a factor, it is not an excuse for failure.

THE HOPE GAP

The first gap that parents need to fill is the hope gap. My brother and I were raised by a single parent, Claudette Calhoun Burton, in a house with our grandparents. By today's definition, we would be considered homeless. Our mom was a teacher. We were poor, but did not know it. Mom instilled in us every day that if our minds could conceive it and in our hearts, we believed it, then we could achieve it. We grew up in the sixties. My mom knew that life for two Black boys wouldn't be a crystal stair, so she gave us this hope and a burning desire for excellence. Children learn what they live, so the quality of education that a child gets is in part due to the quality of parenting. Mom closed the hope gap by allowing us to have a dream, and to dream big.

I believe that the words of Dr. Martin Luther King, Jr.'s "I Have a Dream" are as real and relevant in 2020 as they were in 1963. He said:

> *Now is the time to make real the promises of democracy. Now is the time to rise from the dark and desolate valley of segregation to the sunlit path of racial justice. Now is the time to lift our nation from the quicksand of racial injustice to the solid rock of brotherhood. Now*

is the time to make justice a reality for all of God's children.

It would be fatal for the nation to overlook the urgency of the moment. This sweltering summer of the Negro's legitimate discontent will not pass until there is an invigorating autumn of freedom and equality. Those who hope that the Negro needed to blow off steam and will now be content will have a rude awakening if the nation returns to business as usual.

Dr. King's words are as true now as they were then for he says, "The marvelous new militancy which has engulfed the Negro community must not lead us to a distrust of all white people, for many of our white brothers, as evidenced by their presence here today, have come to realize that their destiny is tied up with our destiny. And they have come to realize that their freedom is inextricably bound to our freedom. We cannot walk alone."

In his speech, he suggested that if America is going to be a great nation, freedom must ring for everyone. So, what does freedom look like in the board room, the public, private and charter schools, the universities and community colleges? Are we willing to think and rethink why we do what we do in the name of education and then make the necessary changes to truly provide liberty and justice for all?

Throughout these pages, my goal has been to present evidence so by the end of each chapter, you will know something, feel something and do something. Other than mentioning The Rensselaerville Institute, I've tried not to mention any organizations, schools or school systems explicitly. However, I would not be a good teacher if I didn't provide an example of a school system and superintendent that has led the way by making the changes that are mentioned in this book and provide us a path forward.

To maintain context and provide clarity on how to move forward in the work that needs to be done, I will state the applicable frame (Structural, Humanistic, Political, Symbolic or a combination).

Allow me to share with you the story of Superintendent Alberto Carvalho. He has served as the Superintendent of Miami-Dade County Schools for the last twelve years. It is the fourth largest school district in the nation and under his leadership, has received some of the highest awards given to school districts in the nation. He was the keynote speaker at the opening session of training provided by the Florida Department of Education's Bureau of School Improvement, which is where I heard him share how he changed Miami -Dade County Schools from one of the lowest performing school districts to one of the best in the country, achieving a performance letter grade of (A). [Symbolic]

His theme was "From the impossible to the inevitable, there is only one belief, skill and will." He outlined ten things he did to transform his schools and school system and they are as follows:

1. **Leadership Matters.** Be a foundational as well as instructional leader who can build bridges with the community and surrounding schools by making data-driven decisions that create the right set of circumstances which result in a positive culture and inspire others to do so. You can't just say every child can learn but you must believe that every child will learn and have the courage to make the tough decisions, such that it happens. This means putting the right people in the right places and holding them as well as yourself accountable. [Structural and Political]

2. **Teacher Effectiveness/Quality.** Reward teachers for getting results and invest in them through the development of human capital. Effective leaders hire effective teachers by asking them the tough questions such as, can you come out of the trenches and transform the life of a child? Can you connect to children? The single most important factor regarding increased student achievement is the quality of the teacher in the classroom. [Humanistic and Structural]

3. **Equality for everyone will never address the issues of equity.** Schools must be tiered based on their needs so that support can be differentiated to meet their needs. In other words, the schools that need the most support get the most support. Using a data matrix in several key areas, the principals get to present the needs of their schools to he and his cabinet and they in turn, create a rapid action response to address critical issues. Accountability is not just a noun, it is a verb as well. [Humanistic and Structural]

4. **Data-driven decisions are made at all levels.** We must have the courage to peel the onion back and

solve the problems wherever they are. [Structural]

5. **Diversity, Equity and Inclusion are the keys to creating positive environments.** These three principles must be adhered to at all times because they are the catalysts for change. [Humanistic and Political]

6. **Digital Equity for all students is a must to alleviate digital deserts.** Digital deserts often occur in the same places as food deserts. Therefore, the type of support must be adequate to alleviate both. [Humanistic]

7. **Parental Choice.** He offers choice to students by innovating and creating choice through the public-school environment. He has 1000 different choice programs that are aligned to workforce industry in the community, which makes learning contextually relevant. He has created magnet schools at places like the airport, zoo and has a police academy magnet school. [Humanistic, Structural, Political]

8. **Parent Academy.** It was created to teach parents how to be a better supporter of their child's

education and how to ask better questions. How to become a "demand side parent" as opposed to a "supply side parent." Supply side parents send their children to school hoping that it will make them better but demand parents have done the research on which schools offer what and demand that their children get a quality education. It helps parents to professionalize themselves as well as teaching the rules of engagement in the world and workforce. [Humanistic, Structural, Political]

9. **Have Fun.** Take care of yourself. Take time to read. [Humanistic]

10. **Try to get fired.** Work yourself out of a job. Lead from the edge of the precipice. No risk, no reward. Do that which is right, rightful, and righteous for our kids. [Humanistic]

What Superintendent Carvalho did and is doing, was not magic nor is it new but he had the will and passion to get it done. As a superintendent, he is the best of the best because he chose to do what was right, rightful and righteous for children, even it if cost him his job. He really has the blueprint for what true equitable education should be and he did nothing new. He just did what was <u>right</u>.

Likewise, as we move from protest to policy, Americans must have the courage, will, and passion to do that which is right, rightful and righteous for our children. That is the only way we are going to increase life chances for all children. That is the only way that America can be great. Moving from protest to policy requires passion and a plan.

When Superintendent Carvalho spoke, we could feel the passion he has for education and children but he had a plan. Dr. Martin Luther King Jr. was able to face death because of the passion. But he had a plan that if followed, would allow young Black boys and young Black girls to be judged by the content of their character rather than the color of their skin. Like Dr. King, John Lewis Jr, faced almost certain death crossing the Edmund Pettis Bridge because of the passion he had for Black Americans to have liberty and justice, but he had a plan.

In a letter he left to be read posthumously, he said [paraphrased], "We are all complicit when we tolerate injustice. It is not enough to say it will get better by and by. Each of us has a moral obligation to stand up, speak up and speak out. When you see something that is not right, you must say something. You must do something. Democracy is not a state. It is an act, and each generation must do its part to help build what we called the Beloved Community, a nation and world society at peace with itself. Ordinary people with extraordinary vision can redeem the soul of America by getting in what I call, good trouble, necessary trouble." Here is the plan, he said, "Voting and participating in the democratic process are key. The vote is the most powerful nonviolent change agent you have in a democratic society. We must continue to build union between movements stretching across the globe because we must put away our willingness to profit from the exploitation of others."

Let me make it plain, our passion-fueled plan must be that we must intentionally get into "Good Trouble." More specifically, that means as citizens we must vote into office, politicians that have the intestinal fortitude to put aside partisan politics and do what is in the best interest for the poorest among us as well as those with means. As citizens, if they continue to engage in partisan politics, we need to have the gall and gumption to vote them out of office.

Educational leaders must hire people that have a

proven track record of results in the position for which they are hired. Likewise, if there is a deficit in their skill set or a teacher's skill set, then job embedded professional development must be done. The development of human capital has to be more than just a cliché, it must be real, relevant and real world. The days are past for hiring friends, relatives for job security and political posturing. Leaders must do that which is right, rightful and righteous for children. Accountability must be expected by everyone from the school board member to the substitute teacher. Systems and structures must be put in place to provide help, support and measurable progress at all levels. Data must be used to make informed decisions. Data-driven decisions is a cliché often used to absolve leaders from making responsible evidence-based decisions. Saying the data made me do it is not an excuse to make easy decisions. Great leaders use the data to make informed evidence-based decisions that result in plans and processes for successful schools.

This applies to university presidents as well. If our institutions of higher learning, HBCUs and HWIs alike, are going to be a place where we train teachers to get in the trenches and do the hard work of teaching, you must be willing to peel back the onion and make the tough decision to displace unproductive professors. Great leaders know how to lead, follow or get out of the way. Good leaders don't, so strive for greatness.

As parents and guardians, you must hold board members and superintendents accountable for making diversity, equity and inclusion more than just words spoken at a meeting. Education should be the great equalizer. Parents cannot tolerate a system that promotes haves and have not schools because they result in have and have not communities. This can easily be accomplished by ensuring that schools that need the most support get the most support by adopting performance-based budgeting instead of zero-based budgeting.

Like Superintendent Carvalho, Superintendents and school board must build bridges in the business community that create philanthropic trust and give principals the autonomy to do the same thing. It is done by creating parent academies to educate parents on how to support their children's education and become informed citizens with a path for professional growth.

Lastly, it is incumbent upon educational leaders

to have fun. Work hard and play harder. No one will take care of you like you!

To reopen schools and go back into the same debacle we have now, would be miseducation. The structures and systems are already in place for us to make the changes in order to reframe American Education. By saying us, I mean, parents, guardians, teachers, principals, politicians, pastors, superintendents, board members, university presidents and professors. In other words, us is we the people. We the people must work to reframe education so that America can be great. More specifically, to quote the late Senator John Lewis, it is time for us to start getting into some "good trouble" because Senator Kamala Harris was right when she said, "The American dream belongs to all of us."

**Your eight minutes and
forty-six seconds starts now.**

CHAPTER FIVE
REFLECTING ON THE REFRAMING PROCESS

"I stand on the shoulders of a generation of young people of color that are united, that clearly understand that we are suffering from structural racism, institutional racism, and capitalism. We are fighting for survival."
—Rosa Clemente

Know: After reading this chapter, I learned...

_____

_____

_____

_____

_____

_____

_____

_____

Feel: Reading this chapter made me feel...

_____

_____

_____

_____

_____

_____

_____

_____

Do: After reading this chapter, I am committed to the following...

_____

_____

_____

_____

_____

_____

_____

_____

SPECIAL ACKNOWLEDGMENTS

I want to especially thank my professors at Seton Hall University as well as the remarkable educators that I had and have the privilege of working with as an educational leader. Thanks is also extended to Renita Bryant, CEO of Mynd Matters Publishing, as well as her team, for their patience, insight, and commitment to see this project through to completion.

KUDOS to my wife, Wanda, my sons, Benjamin and Zachary, as well as our grandchildren, Brayden, Averee, Aeren, and Brooklynn for constantly encouraging me.

Hopefully, this book will pave the way for a system of education that is truly equitable and equal.

We hope you enjoyed *The Reframing of American Education* and will take a few minutes to leave a review.
Writing a review helps an indie author more than you know!

To learn more, visit the author's website at www.PassionDrivenLeadership.org.